Dancing with Dandelions

The wild rhapsody of Rex Hunt's new work, *Dancing with Dandelions*, stems and grows from its elegiac urgency to save and pass on the many lines and voices – quotes of teachers, scientists, and poets – whose words turned his life around, and whose voices we now need desperately to take to heart. Over a lifetime of doing just that, their vision has become his responsibility – their voices taken up in his own, channelling their joy, wisdom, and passion for our time.

Joseph A Bessler. BA. MTS. PhD
Robert Travis Peake Professor of Theology
Phillips Theological Seminary, Tulsa, OK

In this collation of sixteen reflections, Rex Hunt as advocate of Religious Naturalism – a belief in the capacity of the natural world to inspire a human response – has produced a work that reflects not only these tenets of RN, but as well is a prompting for the reader to a greater commitment to care for Earth. Emanating from Rex's role as a progressive liturgist, they include a myriad of accessible references. *Dancing with Dandelions* is highly recommended to both lay person and practitioner.

David Volk. BA. DipEd.
Retired Uniting Church Minister and Teacher; former Senior Public Servant
Ballarat Vic
David died in March 2025.

In a series of reflective essays around wonder, awe and curiosity, Rex Hunt urges us to rediscover a mystical naturalism that reminds us we are part of nature, not over or beyond nature. We need to be at-home in the universe, not dragged out of this deeply spiritual natural residence into some supernatural mysticism – not "hosannah in the highest" but here. By introducing many writers – some familiar, some less so – Hunt invites us into this "wild faith" by paying attention, rejoicing in our surroundings, and caring for nature, our home. Thank you, Rex, for this timely reminder.

Val Webb. BSc(Hons). BA. PhD
Australian theologian and author
Mudgee NSW

Awe, Wonder,
and a 'Wild' Mystical Naturalism

Dancing with Dandelions

Rex A. E. Hunt

COVENTRY
PRESS

Published in Australia by
Coventry Press
33 Scoresby Road
Bayswater VIC 3153

ISBN 9781922589644

Copyright © Rex A. E. Hunt 2025

All rights reserved. Other than for the purposes and subject to the conditions prescribed under the *Copyright Act*, no part of this publication may be reproduced, stored in a retrieval system, or transmitted in any form or by any means, electronic, mechanical, photocopying, recording or otherwise, without the prior permission of the publisher.

Catalogue-in-Publication entry is available from the National Library of Australia
http://catalogue.nla.gov.au

Cover design by Ian James – www.jgd.com.au
Text design by Coventry Press
Set in EB Garamond
Printed in Australia 2025

Contents

Acknowledgments and Thanks	ix
Introduction	xiii

Essays

1.	The Sacred 'Wounderosity' of Nature	1
2.	Beauty, Nature and Religious Sensitivity	12
3.	A 'Wild' Mysticism? Courtship of the Particular	20
4.	Hyacinths, Biscuits... and the Fragrance of Life	33
5.	Festivals, Transience... and Leaves	39
6.	Remembering We Too are Desert Flowers	48
7.	The Landscape is...	55
8.	Looking to Nature: Landscape, Plants and Beauty	63
9.	Cultivating a Culture of Reverence	70
10.	Old Trees, Wonder, and Orwell's Roses	79
11.	Awe and Spirituality of Nature	87
12.	Reverencing Water, Womb of Life	98
13.	Bread, Wine, and the Cosmos	111
14.	Blowing in the '*Ruah*'	124
15.	Cosmic Life... and Death	134
16.	Boney and Spindly! Reviving Liturgy with the Sensuous Textures of Landscape	144

Epilogue	161
Some 'Take-Aways' from Bernard Eugene Meland	167
Combined Bibliography	169

Acknowledgments

*"Mysticism... that approach to life which seeks an emotional relationship
with the vaster order of reality, is the quality-giving medium.
It adds cosmic dimension to human living,
increasing in men, wonder, awe, and wide appreciation.
It evokes the expansive reach toward other creatures of earth,
and thus provides the emotional basis for all attitudes
and habits of conduct that make for the good life.
It... impels them to live magnificently and creatively."*
Bernard Eugene Meland[1]

"A 'Wild' Mysticism? Courtship of the Particular"
• This is an extended essay of an earlier version published in **The Fourth R** 38, 2, (March-April 2025), 17-20, 22, under the title "A Wild Mysticism?" (With permission).

"Looking to Nature: Landscape, Plants and Beauty"
• A shorter version appeared in **Eremos Magazine**, 158, December 2023 (With permission).

"Old Trees, Wonder, and Orwell's Roses"
• Some sections of this essay first appeared in an article in **The Fourth R** 33, 6, (November-December 2020), 3-8, 22, under the title "Old Trees, Stardust, and Moments of Wonder. An Introduction to Religious Naturalism". (With permission).

"Flower Communion Service"
A similar liturgy first appeared in R A E Hunt. *When Progressives Gather Together. Liturgy, Lectionary, Landscapes... And Other*

---

1   Meland. *Modern Man's Worship* 297.

Explorations. Northcote, Morning Star Publishing. 2016. The book is now out of print. Author's rights returned.

The Liturgy itself was shaped from the various published writings and resources of:
Bumbaugh, D. E. "Flower Communion Service" and "A Springtime Service" in C. Seaburg. (ed). *The Communion Book*. Boston. UUMA, 1993.
The St Hilda Community. *The New Women Included. A Book of Services and Prayers*. London. SPCK, 1996.
UUA Worship Web. Boston. <www.uua.org/spirituallife/worshipweb/>
Galston, D. "Liturgy in the Key of Q" in D. Galston. *Embracing the Human Jesus. A Wisdom Path for Contemporary Christianity*. Salem. Polebridge Press, 2012
Vearncombe, E. et al. (ed). *After Jesus Before Christianity. A Historical Exploration of the First Two Centuries of Jesus Movements*. New York. HarperOne, 2021

"Cosmos Liturgy" shaped from the various published writings of:
• Margie Abbott. *Cosmic Sparks. Igniting a Re-Enchantment with the Sacred*. Bayswater. Coventry Press, 2020
• David Bumbaugh. Selected Communion Liturgies published in (ed) Carl Seaburg. *The Communion Book*. Boston. Unitarian Universalist Ministers Association, 1993, plus "Toward a Humanist Vocabulary of Reverence". Boulder International Humanist Institute, Fourth Annual Symposium, Boulder, Colorado. (22 February 2003). <http://www.uua.org/sites/live-new.uua.org/files/documents/bumbaughdavid/humanist_reverence.pdf>
• Elizabeth Johnson. "Deep Incarnation: Prepare to be Astonished", *UNIFAS Conference, Rio de Janeiro*, (7-14 July 2010). <https://sgfp.wordpress.com/2011/02/15/deep-incarnation-prepare-to-be-astonished/>

Acknowledgments

- Bruce Sanguin. "Cosmic Sacrifice" and "Feast of the Cosmos" in *If Darwin Prayed: Prayers for Evolutionary Mystics*. Vancouver. ES Press, 2010
Plus Thich Nhat Hanh, Gretta Vosper, Matthew Fox, Thomas Berry, David Galston, and others... with grateful thanks.

Some Words of Thanks

Thanks to my long-time editor Hugh McGinlay, through seven books. Thanks also to friends and colleagues David Volk, Denise Paton, Gereldine Leonard, Val Webb, Gina Hastings, Joseph Bessler (USA) and James Veitch (New Zealand) – all have read part or all of the original manuscript, and when comments were offered they were encouraging and helpful. But a special mention of Romeo Ellard – our 13-year-old/Year 7 grandson. He too has read sections of this collection! All after having participated in his first philosophy workshop (yes!) and had his interest stimulated. So proud.

To the scholars whose thoughts, books, and personal conversations have aroused in me a continuing curiosity for all things 'natural', my grateful thanks. To those folk who have listened to the oral presentations – in congregations, audiences, and on-line events, your attendance has been much appreciated.

To Dylis McConnell-Hunt my partner/spouse of 60 years... my late brother Ian used to reckon she deserved a medal from the (then) Queen! To Laurie Michell and the other 12 blokes of our 'Tuesday Coffee Club' who attempt to keep me grounded as we care for each other while seeking to change the world. Blokes caring for blokes! To all three grandchildren: Elsie, Romeo and Lenna as they begin the transitions leading to a reflective life. Not just learning to 'think', but 'thinking things through'. And their parents: Rowena, John, Brendan. Hugs to you all.

To overseas colleagues: John Churcher, Andrew Pratt, John Ramsbottom, Gretta Vosper, James Macdonald, Bruce Sanguin, Sir Lloyd Geering, Glynn Cardy, Keith Rowe, James Veitch, David Felten, B. Brandon Scott, Joseph Bessler, Hal Taussig, David Galston, Tom Hall, Robert Miller, Jerry Stone, Wesley Wildman, Michael Zimmerman, and an around-the-BBQ chat with Ty Inbody in 1993 in Dayton, OH; and when he was alive, Bishop John Shelby Spong – for friendship, encouragement, advice and support over a span of 30 years.

And gratitude to colleagues in the Australian 'progressive' religion movement as together we have challenged the institutions: Val Webb, Jonathon Rea, George Stuart, Ian Pearson, Rod Pattenden, Linda Pure, Paula Morelli, Ralph Catts, David Merritt, David Volk,[2] John Cranmer, John W. H. Smith,[3] Rod Peppiatt, Alexandra Sangster, Margaret Mayman, Richard Carter, Coralie Ling, Wes Hartley, Richard Smith, Ann Gray, Norman Habel, Jeremy Greaves, Lorraine Parkinson, Greg Jenks, Paul Inglis.

---

2   David Volk died March 2025.
3   John Smith died 16 October 2024.

Introduction

> *"The religious response, in its pure form,*
> *is the aesthetic attitude projected to cosmic ends.*
> *It is the deep, elemental, appreciative response of creatures*
> *toward vast and mysterious environings,*
> *out of which their world of life has arisen and is sustained."*
> Bernard Eugene Meland

As we come to the end of the first quarter of the twenty-first century, we are continuing to be met with bold new challenges. And leading some of those challenges is the relationship between religion and environmental science which demands relearning – even reconstruction – of our religious orientation.

This reconstruction is especially needed by the religion called Christianity which has largely ignored the reality that we are Earthlings. And where supernaturalism and its twin, fundamentalism, are continuing to flex their muscles and seek to undermine society and its institutions: religion, education, governance, politics – as we have experienced them, and our role and responsibilities as humans embedded in the larger Earth community. Earth... one amazing domain where all components are connected in a wondrous web.

> The intrinsic wonder of this planet and all its interconnected mysteries must now be affirmed, and the right of all living entities (including Earth) to live fully must now be endorsed by legal, political, and religious bodies.[4]

★★★

---

4   Habel. *Rainbow of Mysteries* 93

The underlying theme of these essays is the place of nature in religion. A 'wild' faith to be exact. My particular interest goes back to the time when, as a theological student in Melbourne in the 1960s, some senior students introduced me to American empirical/process theology. Initially, I was animated by the liberal theology of Henry Nelson Wieman (1884–1975) – his naturalistic theism made possible a theistic stance without the supernatural God – but years later I added in a more intentional way the 'poetic' empirical theology – the 'early' years (1930–1937) that is – of Bernard Eugene Meland (1899–1993). It is with the latter's theology – Meland called his stance 'mystical naturalism' – and those whom Meland has influenced, that I now spend many reading and writing and speaking hours. And it is the shaping content of this collection.

Over the years, my interest has become more like a passion… sharing with others 'mystical naturalism' as a religious orientation, or Religious Naturalism (RN) as much of it is called today. Nature is so significant that all our beliefs must be reformulated so as to take nature into account. And that includes exploring the 'wild' voice print of the earthling sage we call Jesus/Yeshu'a.[5]

> Born of a woman… and the Hebrew gene pool, [he] was a creature of earth, a complex unit of minerals and fluids, an item in the carbon, oxygen, and nitrogen cycles, a moment in the biological evolution of this planet. Like all human beings, he carried within himself the signature of the supernovas and the geology and life history of the Earth…[6]

An earthling sage, formally unschooled, who left oral discourses – brief sayings and secular stories with a twist in their tail, discussing the common natural 'stuff' of life, devoid of 'religious' significance…

---

5   See Hunt. "In Celebration of a 'wild' Faith: Jesus in the Australian Landscape" in G. C. Jenks (ed.) *Interfaith Afterlives of Jesus. Jesus in Global Perspective 2*. Westar Studies. Eugene. Cascade Books, 2023.
6   Johnson. "Deep Incarnation", 4–5.

Introduction

A possible Jesus situated in his historical circumstances of Galilee of the Roman Province of Palestine in the early years of the first century who said and did things of his time. A Jesus who was far away from a *supernatural* 'white' Jesus of the creeds and doctrines and christological baggage – in biblical scholarship called the dogmatic Jesus – who came from the sky, and "was used to colonise countries around the world, engage in holy wars, and enforce enslavement and genocide."[7]

Following other theologians, I have often made the claim that religion is born out of a sense of wonder and awe. We will recover our sense of wonder and our sense of sacred only if we appreciate the universe beyond ourselves. The landscape. The sky above, the earth below. The grasses, the flowers, the forests, the fauna... Nature. The miracle of each moment awaits our sensual wonder. Thus the most imperative undertaking in life – call it one's religion or philosophy of life – is the endeavour to adapt oneself courageously to the facts of existence and thus prepare to live the life of integrity.

Whether or not we believe there is something more, that is (with or without the god G-o-d), nature is so significant that all our beliefs must be reformulated so as to take nature into account. We don't need to look for rarified *super*natural revelation. We simply need to recognise the sacrality of everything around us. And to heed the warnings about our current lifestyle options. Ecologist and marine biologist Rachel Carson (1907–1964), author of the 1962 influential book *Silent Spring*, wrote:

> The history of life on earth has been a story of interaction between living things and their surroundings. To a large extent, the physical form and the habits of the earth's vegetation and its animal life have been molded by the environment. Considering the whole span of earthly time, the opposite effect, in which life actually modifies its surroundings, has been relatively slight. Only within the

---

[7] Grace Ji-Sun Kim. Cato Lecturer, Uniting Church Assembly July 2024.

moment of time represented by the present century has one species – man – acquired significant power to alter the nature of his world.⁸

About Mystical Naturalism

This collection seeks to offer and respond to what Bernard Meland – an important but oft-times neglected theologian – in the 1930s called mystical naturalism (which later was incorporated more generally into religious naturalism). Indeed, his book *Modern Man's Worship* (1934) was a core defence of the thesis that religion, in its basic form, is an appreciative awareness or aesthetic response to cosmic reality. In my often-used quotation by Meland...

> Have you ever communed in the first person with this total wealth of living life about you? Have you ever stood with awe and wonder before the unbounded totality of all reality – this ongoing process we call the universe, feeling your own intimacy with all its life, thrilling with the realization of the magnitude of that relationship, relating you to all the world's life, past, present and future? If you have, you have experienced first-hand religion.⁹

Tyron Inbody, a constructive theologian in his own right, and who has studied Meland's theology over many years, writes, quoting Meland:

> *naturalistic* 'in the sense that I take the universe, described by the sciences, as the natural home of man, and the environment in which he must fulfil his life'; it is *mystical* 'in the sense that I affirm the possibility of having religious relations with the *Cosmic Phase* of man's world'.¹⁰

---

8 Carson. *Silent Spring*, 5
9 Meland. *Modern Man's Worship*, 234.
10 Inbody. Constructive Theology of Bernard Meland, 50.

Introduction

Writing several years later and found among his 'unpublished papers' Meland expanded his initial thoughts...

> means understanding this human response to life's meanings which the genuinely poetic and aesthetic person reveals with a view to discerning just what that kind of human response can convey of these deeper meanings that lie about us in everyday living like a haze, or a mist, confounding our vision because we do not have eyes to see what is so full of radiance and wonder. It means a contemplative grasp of what we live with, instead of sheer utility, or scrutiny. Here the modern mystic can help to restore to us in our religious thinking what the poet and artist have provided for aesthetic thinking.[11]

Mysticism is a human affair. It is human beings who are mystics. Mysticism in past times was supernaturalist. Modern mysticism is naturalistic, a celebration of life, responsive to awe and wonder all around us and in nature. If we are to find the mysticism of natural experience, we must avail ourselves of nature. A mossy stone pitted by wind and rain. A tree alive in its soil. A dragonfly nestled on a blade of wetland grass. Creeds and codes are not religion.

Over the years, mystical naturalism – being at-home in the universe – has been shaped by the likes of Bernard Meland, Henry Nelson Wieman, Karl Peters (1939-2025), Jerome Stone and others. The basic question for Meland was: can humans be at-home in the universe without cultivating illusions? "Whenever supernaturalism has influenced human thought," writes Meland,

> man has conceived his life on earth as only a temporary residence in a vale of tears. His real home was in the skies. The tragedy of supernaturalism has been that it has lured man away from the universe. It has left him hostile, fearsome, or indifferent to the great life that surges through him and through his fellow creatures.[12]

---

11 Meland. "Mysticism in Modern Terms", 86-87.
12 Meland. *Modern Man's Worship*, 146-147.

So, who is or might be, a mystical/religious naturalist?' I offer five (5) general 'wisdom principles' (the religious bit) coupled with six (6) general short statements (the naturalist bit), shaped with the flavour of a 'new' theo*poetics* Alves-style mood – all as a possible guide.

A **mystical/religious** naturalist:

i. understands 'sacred events' are not manifestations of something deeper of another realm, but rather a revised insight into the importance of things;
ii. explores more than one religious tradition, especially in this pluralistic day and age;
iii. seeks to discover the counterpoint between divergent themes within a religious tradition rather than glossing over them;
iv. acknowledges such exploration needs to go beyond the 'official' interpretations stated by any tradition – boundaries need to be pushed, and where necessary, reconstructed;
v. encourages an 'openness' or dialogue... where both the self and the tradition is challenged to learn and to grow.

A mystical/religious **naturalist**:

i. holds a naturalist view of how things are in the world;
ii. sees themselves as religious (or spiritual), in non-traditional ways, as they absorb the wonder of being alive and the order and beauty of the cosmos;
iii. asks "What is?" and "What matters?" questions, seeking wisdom from natural (rather than *super*natural) sources, including ritual, art, poetry, story, music, dance, philosophy, science and world religions – appreciating ancient stories as metaphor or myth, rather than as literally true;
iv. respects things that clearly matter, such as ecological stability and social justice;

v. seeks to learn from and care about the natural world, including its humankind;
vi. celebrates a doctrine of incarnation which suggests the universe itself is continually incarnating itself in "microbes and maples, in humming birds and human beings... inviting us to tease out the revelation contained in stars and atoms and every living thing".[13]

About the Title

Why *dandelions*? Why indeed! Dandelions[14] grew in our front nature strip – not sure we could call it a lawn, but it was a great neighbourhood cricket pitch – at our family home in Lynott Street, Horsham, and proved to be hardy and very resilient beings. Plus, as I am writing this essay, I can see there are six dandelion[15] flowers currently on display in the grassed area at the front of my son's flooring showroom on the New South Wales Central Coast.

Dandelions have one of the longest flowering seasons of any plant. But they get a bad name as they are officially classed as weeds in several Australian states.[16] They get on gardeners nerves! And like all weeds, it is deemed they should be removed, eradicated. A bit like mosquitoes and cockroaches. Reviled creatures! Mmm. Perhaps we need to stop for a moment and be reminded of Ralph Waldo Emerson's comment when he said that a weed was a plant whose virtues have not yet been discovered.

---

13 Bumbaugh. "Toward a Humanist Vocabulary of Reverence" (2003).
14 Not to be confused with a similar yellow and black plant called Cape Weed... a member of the sunflower family. It has also been claimed that the dandelion is the only flower that represents the three celestial bodies of the sun (yellow flower), the moon (the puff ball) and the stars (dispersing seeds).
15 The name 'dandelion' is taken from the French word "dent de lion" meaning lion's tooth, referring to the coarsely-toothed leaves
16 In Victoria, New South Wales, South Australia, Tasmania and Western Australia.

As weeds, dandelions are hardy and resilient. Products of evolution. They succeed where other plants fail. As flowers, dandelions play their own role in the great web of life. A role which is independent of human feelings about them and local government by-laws. To just think eradication is to do dandelions an injustice. The fact is they do humans a great service. Not only are they safe to eat but I am assured they also provide a range of health benefits... a rich source of beta carotene and polyphenol compounds, both of which may neutralise harmful free radicals and protect against chronic disease. All parts of a dandelion plant are edible, from the top of the yellow flower down to the roots. While the green leaves can make a healthy addition to salads, sandwiches, omelettes and more.

But that's not all!, as the TV salespeople say. They help surrounding plants get much-needed nutrients as well as aerate the soil. When they have finished flowering, they let slip their withered outer shawl and emerge as 'a white-haired senior' – those wispy whites are called *pappi* – and will sail in the wind to make new roots in the earth elsewhere. Dandelions are masters of survival. They are sensing their environment and responding to their environment in incredibly sophisticated ways. So it seems fitting to promote dandelions to their rightful place in nature. And not just because of their instrumental value to human beings, but also for their intrinsic beauty as beings and part of nature. An important and 'intelligent' – be it a fleeting – part of nature.

> If we accept flowering is by its nature a fleeting occurrence, then we are more likely to recognise each bud as a victory, each blossom as a triumph... to relish the beauty in front of us, and the almost infinite possibilities contained in every hour, or a single breath.[17]

---

17 Baird. *Phosphorescence* 112.

Introduction

Professor of environmental studies and member of the Citizen Potawatomi Nation, Robin Wall Kimmerer, says that when she works with plants similar to dandelions she has 'photosynthesis envy'.

> The ability to take these non-living elements of the world – air and light and water – and turn them into food that can be shared with the whole rest of the world, to turn them into medicine that is medicine for people and for trees and for soil – and we cannot even approach the kind of creativity that they have.[18]

Then about three weeks after a couple of drafts of this Introduction, I again picked up James Bridle's book *Ways of Being* and started to flick through the chapter "Seeing like a Planet" where he too challenges us to 'pay attention'. Pay attention to what is happening within the environment. Pay attention to the trees and their leaves... to the voices of the birds. To the changing water's edge, to the budding bougainvillea, to the rocks, to the build-up of silt in rivers. Pay attention... to nature. To climate change. Hotter summers. Fiercer storms. More severe bushfires. "We know that climate change is occurring, but for a long time it felt to many of us like an abstraction". Pay attention to actual changes. To predicted changes.

Bridle tells a story. How he cut a bamboo stick 115 centimetres long and laid it down on a scrubby patch of lawn, "one end next to a tough-looking dandelion, the other pointed northwards". Then he dug up the dandelion at one end of the stick and replanted it at the other end. "A small step for humans, but quite a leap for the dandelion". Why? Why 115 centimetres? He explains:

> the global mean velocity of climate change is about 0.42 kilometres per year. Divide that by 365, and you get 115 centimetres – the length of my bamboo rod. That's the

---

[18] Kimmerer. "The Intelligence of Plants' 8.

distance the dandelion has to move, *every single day*, just to live in the same conditions... Understanding this velocity is crucial to the survival of life on Earth. It is the speed we need to move in order for the conditions around us to stay the same.[19]

The climate crisis is real! So what is to become of that dandelion...

or those roses, or that oak, or indeed all the other plants, those vegetal souls, as climate change sweeps inevitably and irreversibly across the face of the planet, at a relentless 115 centimetres a day?[20]

As beings that are part of nature, dandelions are at-home *in* nature. If human beings are to survive, we too need to be at-home in nature not claim to be *over* nature. At home... with appreciative awareness and reverence. By slowing down enough to appreciate the lives and forms which surround us every day and may even want to engage with us. And if we are to promote change, especially in such causes as tackling climate change – a demise we appear to be hastening – and the gas and fossil fuel[21] lobby groups sponsored by the likes of Repsol, Shell, ExxonMobil, Chevron, BP, and their mates in Silicon Valley developing AI (artificial intelligence

---

19 Bridle. *Ways of Being*, 120, 122 (Italics in original). See https://doi.org/10.1038/nature08649
20 Bridle. *Ways of Being*, 123.
21 Australia is one of the world's largest exporters of fossil fuels. While this coal and gas is burned beyond our borders, the climate-warming carbon dioxide (CO_2) emissions affect us all... Australia is the world's third-largest fossil fuel exporter, after Russia and the United States. But it gets worse when the fuel is used. Australia exports so much coal that our nation is the second-largest exporter of fossil fuel CO_2 emissions. Unfortunately, just when we need to be cutting emissions, Australia is doubling down on fossil gas extraction mainly for LNG production and export. Federal government policies enabling and/or promoting continued high fossil fuel exports threaten to sabotage international efforts to limit global warming. (Bill Hare. *The Conversation*, 13 August 2024).

algorithms), then *we may need to* get on the Empire's nerves, period! Because the lobby groups and conservative politicians' vision of the future is, in short, no future at all! And would you believe it! All packaged under the heading of 'intelligence'?

Why *dancing*? I first learnt ballroom dancing when I was 15 years young. Even taught a few steps to others. But, much later, I resonated with the power of the dance metaphor in religion, having read Karl Peters' book *Dancing with the Sacred*. The primary challenge of dancing, says Peters, revolves around who leads. And the best kind of dancing according to him is when no one leads, when the leading is a back and forth sharing, when each party responds to the subtle movements, touches, gestures, and words of the other. In the same chapter, Peters claims that Darwinian evolution suggests nature as constantly dancing, due to the continual interactions taking place within the cells of organisms.

> In learning to dance with the natural world around us and with other human beings, we become more alive. This is the big payoff. We become more in tune with ourselves, others, and the natural world. We see more, experience more, enjoy more. We become part of the dance of the sacred – the dance of that system of interactions in the universe and society that brought us into being, that sustains us in our living, and that continually transforms us as part of the ever-changing future.[22]

In an earlier major article, "Storytellers and Scenario Spinners", Peters also explores two metaphors for the process that creates life and guides human thinking: storytelling[23] and dance/music:

> Metaphors of dance and music allow one to deal with the dynamic aspect of evolving nature [or with G-o-d] as continuing creator more effectively than spatial metaphors

---

22 Peters. *Dancing with the Sacred* 51.
23 On storytelling and narrative theology/communication see Hunt, *Please Tell Us Your Stories*, (1993)

or personal metaphors of God as craftsman or designer. Dance and music are temporal and hence allow us to capture irreversible processes involving chance and law in the context of story.[24]

I warm to all these metaphors.[25] To Peters' general 'music' I would specify 'jazz' – the music created by a system of interacting players... some players provide the beat, others add variations on a theme. Freestyle. I would also want to add 'country music' to my styles list – the music of emotion and story, and a six-hour Sunday night radio program I put together for a couple of years 45 years ago in country Victoria. All such metaphors are shaped by an aesthetic mood. Emotionally oriented in the universe. "The human heart would suffocate if it were restricted to logic," reminds Amos Wilder.[26]

And speaking of story... Brazilian theologian Rubem Alves (1933–2014) offers a powerful *'theopoetic'* gem. It puts goosebumps on one's arm. After telling a particular story about a dead man who was washed up on the shores of a local village,[27] Alves asks:

> Did you understand the story? I hope not. If you did, it is because you have succeeded in digesting it. But stories are like poems; they are not to be understood. Something which is understood is never repeated. Understanding exhausts the word. It leaves the word empty with nothing left to be said. Once the word is understood it is reduced to silence. But a story is like a sonata, a love embrace, a poem, a sunset: we want them to be repeated, because their savor is inexhaustible.[28]

---

24 Peters. "Storytellers..." 487, Note No. 5.
25 On story, see my essay "Please Tell Us Your Stories" in this collection.
26 Wilder. *Theopoetic* 75.
27 The story is in "Please Tell Us Your Stories", this collection.
28 Alves. *The Poet, The Warrior, The Prophet* 23-24.

Introduction

About the Book

The over-all purpose of this collection is to be an invitation (rather than an argument) for mystical naturalism. The setting of some of the essays started life as an oral presentation in a study group or a pub. Or even as a Sermon/Address in a Church or Fellowship, especially at Spirit of Life Unitarian Fellowship in North Sydney (NSW). Others were Reflections on what I was reading or experiencing at the time. But, unlike in previous books I have written, I have not continued to present them using what I called 'oral writing'. Just single column print text this time, but retaining sectional cameos in most of the essays. Cameos... because I have attempted to offer each as an order of *experience* – shaped more like a mud map, moving horizontally (process) – than as an order of *ideas* – like an office building, brick upon brick, vertically (structure).

I also envisage this collection as a continuation to my previous book *Seasons and Self*, only this time I have viewed 'being at-home' in nature via the lens of mystical naturalism as shaped by Bernard Meland back in the 1930s – whom I reckon was way ahead of his time – with an added touch of support offered by religious humanist Kenneth L. Patton (1911–1994) and celtic philosopher, poet, Irish bard, John O'Donohue (1956–2008), among many others. As the essays have all been given a life at different times and places with various audiences, this has resulted in several having within them some overlap of material from other presentations/essays. While I have edited out some such material, where there is overlap it is because the context requires their expression. But as I have said on other occasions: "I have done so taking my lead from Indigenous author Bruce Pascoe who claims that sometimes you need to repeat something a hundred times before a bell rings in the colony".[29] My hope is, with the publication of this collection, others will

---

29 See Bruce Pascoe. *Black Duck. A Year at Yumburra* (2024)

resonate with what has been offered by this 'minor-league' player, and delve more fully into the various writings and authors with whom I have shared my journeys. They deserve added attention and appreciation.

Unconcluding Words...

We need to be encouraged to explore radical new or different approaches, because it is by such trackless places and experiences that we can touch the sacred lurking below the surface of our natural experiences. For me, mystical naturalism is a radically different approach compared to what continues to be served up in many theological courses, especially in Australia.

How we view nature is important as John O'Donohue has highlighted: for instance, it makes a huge difference whether you believe your geographical location is 'alive' or 'dead'. We are not on the outside looking in. We are part of nature. Our very existence as Earthlings – being at-home in the universe – is rooted in the fundamental processes of the universe itself. Which makes the fact that Earth has been radically altered by just one species, the human species, all the more depressing.

So I return to the wisdom of the Meland epigraph (written several decades ago) at the beginning of this Introduction – words for a 'nature' journey of awe, wonder and mystical naturalism... addressed to the 'body' by art and story. Because the insight of the naturalistic mystic adds the insight that comes with the sensitivity of a poet or the artist – an approach of openness and wide receptivity... with great emotion and feeling. To those epigraph words I add a challenge from geologian and priest Thomas Berry (1914–2009):

> We need to move from a spirituality of alienation from the natural world to a spirituality of intimacy with the natural world, from a spirituality of the divine as revealed in the written scriptures to a spirituality of the divine as revealed

in the visible world about us, from a spirituality concerned with justice only for humans to a spirituality of justice for the devastated Earth community... The sacred community must now be considered the integral community of the entire universe and, more immediately, the integral community of the planet Earth".[30]

Plus some poetic flair from religious humanist Kenneth Patton (1911–1994) seventy years before the days of inclusive language and environmental studies:

> Our bodies are native to the soil and the sea. The recognition of bare feet in the grass, of the finger crumbling the loam, of the body in the warm water, is a mystical communion of the flesh with the medium of its own composition. Compositions as we are of clay and water and sunshine, our bodies make and remake themselves continuously out of the air, water and soil about them. This living intercourse is the measure of our true at-homeness.[31]

Mystical naturalism will not solve all the environmental issues. But its concern for an 'appreciative awareness' – reading the landscape – and its recognition of a 'courtship of the particular' – *that* tree, *those* flowers, *these* birds, *the* air we breathe, *those* ancient rocks – provides a general direction toward widening the sphere of influence, both in the community and with particular beings. Easily overlooked, this world is always already there... the clouds overhead, a butterfly gliding by, wildflowers bouncing in the breeze, the ground underfoot. Intersubjective world. Life-world. Of immediate importance is embracing the magic of wilderness, considering our shared position in the cosmos, and the excitement of exploring nature. Awe experiences. A love of nature.

So, to a 'wild' faith shaped by mystical naturalism. Mystical naturalism as embraced and gifted by one, Bernard Eugene

---

30 Berry. *Sacred Universe* 133.
31 Patton. *Man's Hidden Search* 55.

Meland... where his suggestions for moral/ethical living shaped by an appreciative sensibility included: (i) keep a growing edge; develop sensitivities which enable one to be open to the signs and symbols of many varying experiences; (ii) cultivate an inquiring spirit; make a distinct effort to keep an attitude of open wonderment, and (iii) participate fully in life; the integrity of a post-critical naiveté will provide something of the poet's discriminating vision...

> [R]eligion in its essential nature is an aesthetic experience of profound proportion. Its meaning and value, therefore, will best be understood and cherished when it is taken with the arts to be an appreciative response to reality; when its concepts are viewed as aesthetic forms, not as science; its words, poetry, not prose; its chief end appreciation and devotion, not inquiry, industry, or control.[32]

Only by being deeply *here*, in and of this *place*, can we be palpably connected to every *other* place.

Summer 2025

Rex A. E. Hunt, *MSc(Hons). GradDipCommMgt*
Birthed on Jardwadjali Country

Retired on Darkinjung Country

---

32 Meland. "Art, Religion and the Cultural Mood" 122-123.

1

The Sacred 'Wounderosity' of Nature

"The galaxies and stars, those nuclear fusion furnaces of the cosmos, still ignite a resonance with something in our being. Creation and destruction are continuities, and we ourselves are glowing with energy waves from the nuclear lights."
Paul Fleischman

My iphone pinged so I knew I had a message. Checking, I saw it was a post from a colleague on the Religious Naturalist Association blog, so I checked it out. It was on prayer. Mmm. Five types of prayer to be exact which he styled some years ago as: 'Wow', 'Thanks', 'Oops, 'Help', 'Yes'. Intrigued, I decided to check it out further:

> prayer begins with the sense of awestruck wonder at life, the universe, and everything. I mean, have you seen this place? It's *amazing*. We've got protons, nebulae, the Big Bang, quantum mechanics, evolution, trees, mountains, sunsets, sex, Van Gogh, Shakespeare, Mother Teresa, single malt scotch, and the Beatles. If you're not saying 'wow' to life at some level, then you're not really paying attention.[33]

★★★

The year was 1931. Not long home from post graduate studies in Germany at the University of Marburg with "the foremost theologian and mystic"[34] Rudolf Otto (1869–1937), and still

---

33 J. Barrett Lee. "Praying Toward Yes" on *Hopping Hadrian's Wall*, 22 November 2013.
34 Inbody. *Constructive Theology*, 15.

shaping his version of 'mystical naturalism',[35] a young American theologian, Bernard Eugene Meland (1899–1993), in his first academic/teaching appointment, penned an article called "The Worship Mood". In that article, he wrote:

> Have you ever communed in the first person with this total wealth of living life about you? Have you ever stood with awe and wonder before the unbounded totality of all reality – this ongoing process we call the universe, feeling your own intimacy with all its life, thrilling with the realization of the magnitude of that relationship, relating you to all the world's life, past, present and future? If you have, you have experienced first-hand religion.[36]

I have shared this quote on several occasions, both in oral presentations and in various writings, and, as you will find, including in this collection of essays, because I believe it is an important observation. While his gendered pronouns grate somewhat now, it is also my hope it might offer a clue as to what contemporary mystical naturalism 90 years later might look and feel like. Not in the occult, misty sense, but in the sense that it claims the roots of human life go into the universe itself "and that in all that we are – biological organisms, mental attainments, and social institutions – we are true children of the earth".[37] It should now be at the centre of any contemporary discussion on spirituality.

Meland had not long spent 12 months (1928–29) as an American-German exchange student at the University of Marburg, "embracing the alluring mystical renascence of Rudolf Otto" (1869–1937) whose book *The Idea of the Holy* had been termed 'as much a turning point in the study of religion as was Darwin's *Origin of the Species* in the study of physical science'.[38] Just prior to

---

35 Meland saw his work as a continuation of the work of Gerald Birney Smith, his mentor and former professor.
36 Meland, "The Worship Mood", 665. Also in *Modern Man's Worship*, 234.
37 Inbody. *Constructive Theology*, 48.
38 Meland. *Modern Man's Worship*, 133.

Otto's retirement, Meland enrolled in his final class. Later in his 1979 intellectual autobiography Meland recounted:

> Although I re-read much of Otto's *Idea of the Holy* and his *Religious Essays – A Supplement to The Idea of The Holy*, I gave more attention to his efforts in the liturgical movement that was evoking widespread attention at the time. A considerable portion of my first book, *Modern Man's Worship*, published in 1934, is devoted to relating to and interpreting that movement, and of exploring particularly Otto's contribution to it.[39]

During this time, Meland considered himself to be a naturalist, philosophically, and a mystic, emotionally. It was because of these two factors that he designated himself during the 1930s to be a 'mystic naturalist'.[40] As others observed:

> It is the 'mystic' character of his naturalistic position that enables Meland's theology to bridge the gap between the scientifically, humanistically oriented view of religion... and the more traditional voices in American religious thought which have come in recent years to dominate...[41]

Prior to his Germany studies, Meland had studied at, among other places, the Divinity School of the University of Chicago[42] under Gerald B. Smith (1868–1929) and Shailer Mathews (1863–1941). Of those liberal years he wrote,

---

39 Meland. "Fifty Years of Religious Inquiry" 7.
40 Peden. *The Chicago School*, 107.
41 Peden. *The Chicago School*, 137,
42 Meland commenced his graduate theological studies in 1925. He was a prominent voice "of liberal student opinion in the Presbyterian Church in the USA, which had emerged from a thirty-two year period when on occasions its General Assembly had adopted several doctrinal items of the fundamentalist agenda. He had a significant personal involvement in an event of large cultural significance: the fundamentalist-modernist controversy" (Towne 1989).

> The most single influence upon my thinking during graduate school days was Gerald Birney Smith. My devotion to him was so complete that for years after his death, I thought of my own work and writing as being a continuation of his labours, which had been cut off so untimely.[43]

During his first teaching appointment at Central College Missouri, Meland expanded some of his initial thoughts:

> My concern with the aesthetic legacy, following my European experience, led me during those early years of teaching to explore a wide range of literature dealing with that idiom. In addition to works on aesthetics, I read extensively in European and American literature, especially poetry, works on aesthetics, including the aesthetics of myth as cultural anthropologists conveyed it. While at Chicago, I had dealt only minimally with this area; but during my early years of teaching, it became a resource which I was to pursue seriously and continuously... Eventually I was to pursue 'the aesthetic-ethic' theme more explicitly within the philosophical idiom, employing what I called 'the appreciative consciousness'.[44]

Years later – after a stint on the faculty of Pomona College in Claremont, California – Meland was appointed to the faculty of the Divinity School of the University of Chicago in 1945 – a School which was seen as "creatively out of step" with other American theological institutions as it had "a commitment to creative scholarship independent of class, rank or privilege". 'Out of step' also because "the scholars who came to teach at the Divinity School... attempted to adapt the scientific method in order to advance the critical study of the Bible and of religious history."[45]

---

43 Quoted in Peden. *The Chicago School*, 106.
44 Meland. As recorded in W. C. Peden. *Life and Thought of Bernard Eugene Meland*, 10.
45 Peden. *The Chicago School*, 10.

Meland's thought was described as rich, complex and nuanced.[46] And his lecture-style was... well it has been told that Joseph Sittler, a fellow faculty member, once described it as:

> When Meland begins to talk, a gentle mist descends upon the room. Shortly, it envelopes everything in a dense fog. The fog always lifts, but when it does all the furniture has been re-arranged! Those who were fortunate enough to be fog bound by Meland did have the furniture of their minds rearranged.[47]

Meland's family were Norwegian Lutheran – part of a large community of Norwegians who emigrated to America during the 1880s and 1890s – and while they were living on the south side of Chicago, attended the local Lutheran Church. Reflecting on those early years, Meland wrote:

> My first encounter with religious stimulus of any kind occurred at age four in a Norwegian Lutheran Church on the South Side of Chicago in a community called Roseland. Our entire neighborhood in those years consisted of Norwegians who had migrated to America during the eighteen eighties and nineties. Most of the men, including my father, were cabinet makers; which may account for the fact that they had settled in an area near The Pullman Car Works.[48]

When they moved away (1910), closer to the country the local Lutheran Church was German-speaking so his parents started

---

46 In casual conversation, Meland was overheard describing himself as "a rebel among process theologians".
47 Williamson. "Bernard E. Meland: What Kind of Theologian?", in *Process Studies 5*, 4, (Winder 1975) 369-390. It has been said by others of Meland that his constructive essays were usually extended soliloquies instead of logical arguments. The form of his theology was more poetic than philosophical, and exhibited more the form of a musical symphony or an artistic photograph than a philosophical treatise or a systematic theology.
48 Meland. As recorded in W. C. Peden. *Life and Thought of Bernard Eugene Meland*, 1.

attending the Presbyterian Church. "So by circumstance more than conviction he became a Presbyterian".[49] Years later, he was ordained a Presbyterian minister despite being challenged on several occasions during his 'trials' – the process Presbyterian candidates went through at Presbytery level prior to ordination – on the Virgin Birth.[50]

Jumping forward some 40 years, Meland was a breath of fresh air to this then Presbyterian theological student (who was also challenged during his 'trials' in the early 1970s by one of his examiners... when I used one particular word, was it spelt 'life' or 'Life'?) And Meland's thinking on the sense of wonder, on nature, and his appreciation of 'the poet', still is! Because he inspired, and later others suggested... There is no good reason to believe that taking nature to heart leaves me or others with any fewer spiritual benefits than taking to heart the teachings of *super*naturalist traditions. If we can go to special places, built by humans, which are designated as sacred, surely we can go to special places, shaped naturally, which are recognised as sacred.

Mystical naturalism seems to have now been submerged under the name *Religious Naturalism* (RN) – described by some as the 'forgotten alternative'. In its RN guise, it has a long pedigree, stretching from Pre-Socratic philosophers into Christian medieval times, through to today where it has been preserved primarily within the academy and small pockets of Unitarian spirituality. Echoing cell biologist Ursula Goodenough at the 2021 IRAS[51] Conference,

> A religious naturalist takes nature to mind and also takes nature to heart – seeking, and finding, deep resources in these understandings for spiritual (inward) and moral (outward) orientation, including an ecomoral orientation.

---

49   Inbody. *Theology of Bernard Meland*, 9
50   Peden. *The Chicago School*, 107.
51   Institute on Religion in an Age of Science.

Religious naturalism is simultaneously a religious and a naturalistic way "of understanding and being oriented morally within the world".[52] It has two central aspects.

(i) Naturalist views, grounded in science, provide a framework for understanding what seems real. These include the grand story or 'drumbeat' – the epic of evolution – that explains the origins of the cosmos and humans, with perspectives from which to consider why we do what we do. We are all one big astonishing family. Brian Swimme and Mary Evelyn Tucker have captured the 'drumbeat' of this story.

> With our empirical observations expanded by modern science, we are now realising that our universe is a single immense energy event that begun as a tiny speck that has unfolded over time to become galaxies and stars, palms and pelicans, the music of Bach, and each of us alive today... This story has the power to awaken us more deeply to who we are. For just as the Milky Way is the universe in the form of a galaxy, and an orchid is the universe in the form of a flower, we are the universe in the form of a human. And every time we are drawn to look up into the night sky and reflect on the awesome beauty of the universe, we are actually the universe reflecting on itself.[53]

(ii) Religious orientation includes spiritual responses, which can include feelings of appreciation, gratitude, humility, reverence and joy at the wonder of being alive. It also includes moral responses, involving values rooted in nature – to seek justice and cooperation among social groups and balance in ecosystems.

Wonderosity[54] and awe when contemplating the immense scale of matter, space and time, is surely appropriate once we realise we belong to something so very far beyond us. Such naturalistic wonder and awe counts as deeply spiritual. In short: Religious

---

52 Hogue, *Promise of Religious Naturalism*, 37.
53 Swimme & Tucker, *Journey of the Universe*, 1-2.
54 Sam Keen crafted the word 'wonderosity - combining 'wonder' with 'curiosity'.

Naturalism, or as Meland called it, 'mystical naturalism' features a blending of world-views and ideas that explores trackless places and experiences which are different from most traditional expressions of religion. Deep attunement. Deep knowledge. Honouring nature all the way down.

In Meland's interpretation of empiricism, he sought a richer, thicker form of experience. In his 1953 book *Faith and Culture*, he suggested that the sense of wonder can best be envisaged as (i) open awareness, (ii) appreciative awareness, and (iii) creative awareness.[55] Expanded, *open awareness* is to go beyond the habit or routine of one's usual behaviour; to introduce a new dimension of response. *Appreciative awareness* is to move beyond simple awareness to knowing the reality out there in their own right. *Creative awareness* means simply "wonder becoming a creative force"; a form of energy affecting, and at times, action, that can become "a transformative power of social magnitude, and can thus be translated into civic and political energies".[56]

But where to start personally? Start with your own life. With the 37.2 trillion cells of your body that are converting energy to make protein right now so you can read these words and see other colleagues. Or... with the awareness that the body you are carrying around now won't be the body you'll be carrying around three, five, seven years from now. It will have completely rebuilt itself from the inside out.

If you want to know where the environment is, just feel yourself. The skin is not a wall around us. The skin, the lungs, the digestive tract are permeable membranes designed to let the environment in. We ignore the environment at our peril.

It may be one thing to know the most common component of sand is silicon dioxide in the form of quartz. It's another, to walk

---

55   Meland. *Faith and Culture*, 172.
56   Meland. *Faith and Culture*, 175.

The Sacred 'Wounderosity' of Nature

along Ocean Beach (NSW) near sunset, with the sand squelching between your toes as waves dance around your ankles! Or... spend autumn – the season of beauty and decline – in Canberra (ACT), amid all the coloured maple leaves, fitting of an artist's palette. Nature scatters the seeds that will bring new growth in the spring... Yet spoiled by the awareness that, every year, autumn is becoming more silent! Death amidst life!

Or... take a three-year-old child (maybe your grand-daughter or grandson) for a walk along a wetlands track. Don't plan to be in a hurry. Every twig. Every muddy pool of water. Every duck or small lizard to cross your path. Every dragonfly will be an occasion for closer 'looking' and 'excitement' and 'wonder'.

The miracle of each moment awaits our sensual wonder. Hosannah! Not in the highest, but right here. Right now. This.[57] Horizontal transcendence. Natural not *super*natural. An experience animated by a sense of wonder, belonging, and relatedness. At the base of all of our knowledge is not certainty, but wonder. Allow yourself to be shaped by this creativity. This wonder. Webs of culture, life and cosmos. Together they are expressions of how we experience the world. To be alive is to experience. We have no inner spiritual development without outer experience, writes Thomas Berry in the 'Introduction' to Kathleen Deignan's book on Thomas Merton's writing on nature.

> When we see a flower, a butterfly, a tree, when we feel the evening breeze flow over us or wade in a steam of clear water, our natural response is immediate, intuitive, transforming ecstatic.[58]

The sacred is *not* a separate '*super*natural' sphere of life, driven by blinding-light revelations. The sacred is that which evokes the depths of wonder. In a time of ecological vulnerability

---

57 Goodenough. *The Sacred Depths...*, 169.
58 Berry. 'Forward' in (ed). Kathleen Deignan, *When the Trees Say Nothing*.

and dislocation of the social fabric, contemporary Religious Naturalism's conceptions of and attitudes toward nature and religiosity have much to commend it. Especially its willingness to entertain radically new approaches, as it engages with some of the most pressing religious and moral issues at the core of the ecological crisis. And to move beyond traditional religious language that has become brittle and lifeless. Because... "the miracle is not to walk on water. The miracle is to walk on the green Earth in the present moment, to appreciate the peace and beauty that is available now".[59]

The chief mark of 'religion' according to philosopher William Ernest Hocking (1873–1966) is not unity but fertility. Religion is the 'mother' of all the great cultural interests of human life. But it lives only while we are making it up. While our imaginations and creative juices are firing and we are generating – *crafting* – new angles, new narratives, new metaphors within the particular context of the moment because these things are liberating. Thus the task of religious faith and the purpose of religious life today is to re-read what is going on in the world. To acknowledge the world as a wondrous place, but not too wondrous to be made better, more humane...

> [T]o re-connect to those purposes and values that, in our best collective judgment, through the critical examination of faith, will most truly and effectively inform our negotiations of what's going on in the pivotal twilight between the religious moral present and future.[60]

Is nature enough? Nature does not provide for complete and final fulfilment of our deepest desires and longings. Neither does it promise perks like eternal life nor an interventionist deity! But it is all we have, and it will have to do... Plus gather people prepared to *interfere* with the ongoing destruction of 'earth mother'. Because (i)

---

59 Thich Nhat Hanh. "Present Moment..."
60 Hogue. *Promise of Religious Naturalism*, 227.

planet Earth "is a one-time project. There is no second chance." And (ii) "we have so intruded ourselves and debilitated the continent in its primordial powers that it can no longer proceed simply on its own."[61]

★★★

Earlier on, I mentioned Kathleen Deignan's edited collection on the nature writings of Thomas Merton. In the Conclusion of that book, Deignan writes:

> Perhaps Merton's writings on nature will awaken the naturalist in us, or the poet, or the creation mystic. Perhaps he will aid us in recovering our senses that were fashioned to be-hold the wonders all around us.[62]

It is to be hoped!

---

61 Berry. *The Sacred Universe*, 175.
62 Brussat review of Deignan's book. https://www.spiritualityandpractice.com/book-reviews/view/5525/when-the-trees-say-nothing

2
Beauty, Nature and Religious Sensitivity

> *"Everybody needs beauty as well as bread, places to play in and pray in, where nature may heal and give strength to body and soul alike."*
> John Muir

In the weeks between my Covid jab in late April 2021 and the first calendar days of the southern hemisphere winter, complete with our flu injections, the 12-year young Japanese Maple (Acer Palmatum) in our front garden (a seedling gift from a mate when we were leaving Canberra) was undergoing a time of transition.

From the gentle chlorophyll green sea-of-life-filled foliage – a miracle of evolution, to its chosen orange and burgundy seven-acutely pointed, lobe leaves... Not an all-at-once process, but a gradual, must-do, life-saving transition as its energy from photosynthesis is diverted to the roots, resulting in autumn technicoloured leaves pirouetting to the ground in a light wind – plop, to become crisp brown litter and our garden's spring fertiliser.[63]

Nature outdoors. Nature approaching the cold of winter clad in a brilliant palette of colours. Nature inviting us to appreciate daily experiences of wonder. As Albert Camus wrote: 'Autumn is a second spring when every leaf is a flower.' We do not just perceive the 'world'. The 'world' gives us something to perceive. A feeling of 'at-home in the universe'... accepting we are creatures of the earth. Yes, a discerning that the universe sustains us, and that there is a

---

[63] The dropping of leaves by deciduous trees is called 'abscission'. It occurs on the cusp between autumn and winter, as part of an arc of growth, maturity and renewal.

functioning creativity within the universe to which we must be related constructively, dare I say 'intimately', in order to fulfil our human nature. As it's been said by others: we are the universe come to consciousness.[64]

When we lose our sense of wonder, we objectivise the Earth as a thing that can be used and abused at our consumeristic whim. There is no shortage of disaster data. The beauty of nature is a fundamental aspect of the human relationship with the wider natural world. In the words of the process philosopher, Alfred North Whitehead, beauty is 'intense harmony'... the guiding lure in every becoming moment. As I stand at my bedroom window on a chilly – sometimes foggy – late autumn morning and gaze out at our self-pruning Japanese Maple, I am struck by three important ingredients from nature: awe, wonder and curiosity. So how should we live in a world overflowing with autumn's natural beauty? Rejoice in it! Care for it! Strive to add our own mite of beauty with whatever talent we possess!

And – we, just perhaps, may be able to move from an appreciation of a maple in its autumn glory, to a sense of the sacredness of that tree, and all of nature, and in doing so, will attempt to protect nature.

★★★

A nineteenth century Scottish-American who was a loving observer of the natural world in all its beauty, wonder and awe, was the inventor, sheepherder, explorer, writer, and naturalist, John Muir (1838–1914). Muir has a reputation as a bit of an ascetic – someone who would plunge into the wilderness "with little more than a crust of bread and a small packet of tea".[65]

---

64 Meland. *Modern Man's Worship*, 156.
65 Brune. "All the Colors", 2015.

He is best known as the co-founder of the Sierra Club – an American environmental organisation, founded in 1892 in San Francisco – and throughout his life was often referred to as 'John of the Mountains'. He is remembered as the patriarchal parent of America's national parks. Especially of his treasured Hetch Hetchy Valley near Yosemite[66] in California. It is said Muir claimed the two greatest moments of his life were when he camped at Yosemite, and when he found the rare orchid calypso (*Calypso borealis*) blooming alone in a Canadian swamp. Less known is the role landscape architect Frederick Law Olmstead (1822–1903) had in shaping and preserving Yosemite, because

> it had value for humans; to be a place surrounded by 'natural scenery... the union of the deepest sublimity with the deepest beauty of nature' – not in any one scene or series of views, but in the whole.[67]

At age 29, while working in a carriage factory "repairing an industrial belt",[68] Muir suffered an injury to the cornea of his right eye which almost blinded him. Shortly after, in appreciation of his regained sight, Muir began his years of barefooted 'wanderlust'. He travelled... no, to be more accurate, he 'sauntered' thousands of miles around the world – USA, Canada, Alaska, Japan, India, Australia to name a few countries. But especially across the whole of America.

One such walk, records Muir's biography, was across the San Joaquin Valley through waist-high wildflowers and into the high country for the first time. Later he would write: 'Then it seemed to me the Sierra should be called not the Nevada, or Snowy Range, but the Range of Light... the most divinely beautiful of all the mountain

---

66   Yosemite was the first tract of wild land set aside by an Act of US Congress, in 1864, 'for public use, resort, and recreation'.
67   Spirn. "Constructing Nature", 92-93.
68   Austin. *Baptised into Wilderness*, 7.

chains I have ever seen'. But ultimately it was California's Sierra Nevada and Yosemite that truly claimed him.

During 1903–1904, Muir went on a 'tree hunting' world tour. He wanted to see the Baobabs, the true cedars of the old world, the Kauri of New Zealand, the strange Araucarias that had so long fascinated him, but, most of all, he wanted to visit Australia "and see if the rumours about the great Eucalyptus were true."[69]

When in Australia, he visited the zoological and botanical gardens and parks in Fremantle, Melbourne and Sydney before heading to New Zealand. The Narbethong Special Purposes Reserve north of Healesville and near Marysville, in Victoria, preserves some of the beech trees, eucalyptus and tree ferns Muir saw on his trip. In a note published by the *John Muir Center*, it says of his NSW stay that Muir travelled inland to see the eucalyptus forests of the Great Dividing Range and took the train from Sydney to Mt Victoria in the Blue Mountains to see the Jenolan Caves...

For Muir, we were born and baptised in wildness. All his life he 'preached' a radical religion of beauty and a 'gospel' of getting outdoors. His radicalism manifested itself in a non-anthropocentric view of nature which saw humans as part of the natural world rather than the centre of it.

> Nature's peace will flow into you as sunshine flows into trees... The winds will blow their own freshness into you, and the storms their energy, while cares will drop off like autumn leaves.[70]

And he rooted his bare-footed sauntering faith in this world and no other.

His oft-repeated exclamation 'Glorious!' wasn't directed to a deity but to the uncontrollable creations of nature.[71]

---

69   Ryan. "Muir and Tall Trees", 1985.
70   Brune. "All the Colors", 2015.
71   Highland. "Muir's Radical Religion" 3.

As the internationally acclaimed Celtic spirituality teacher John Phillip Newell says, Muir's approach to study and observation was eccentric. "This was my method of study," says Muir.

> I drifted about from rock to rock, from stream to stream, from grove to drive... When I discovered a new plant, I sat down beside it for a minute or day, to make its acquaintance and try to hear what it had to say... I asked the boulders I met, whence they came from and whither they were going."[72]

Regarded in his day as an 'orthodox' Christian, Muir was impatient with religion that was 'sectarian' as well as any narrow insistence on dogma, doctrine or confessions.[73] Interestingly, older biographers identified him as a creationist, while modern scholars seem to place him in the evolutionist camp. He personally admired Charles Darwin and even felt compelled to defend his work, understanding evolution to mean not random change but continuous, ongoing creation by a Divine Inventor... A blend of empirical science and Judaeo-Christian metaphysics.[74]

★★★

Margaret Atwood is a Canadian poet, novelist, essayist and environmental activist. She is also the author of the 1985 book on which the TV series *The Handmaid's Tale*[75] is based. In one of her

---

72 Newell. *Sacred Earth, Sacred Soul*, 160.
73 "Muir's natural theology is one of liberation rather than redemption. His is a creation-centered spirituality assuming the goodness of all things natural, wild, and free. No savior is necessary: all we have to do is 'lift up our eyes unto the hills'. In this natural religion there is no original sin and no overwhelming burden of guilt. No world-transforming sacrifice is required. In this sense Muir's new faith is profoundly unChristian." (*Tallmadge* n.d.:71).
74 Limbaugh. "The Nature of John Muir's Religion", 1985.
75 "...the world that postmillennial White Christian nationalists want to bring into reality, and they want to do so 'in the name of God'." (David Galston).

poems which expresses a naturalistic spirituality: 'God is not the voice in the whirlwind. God *is* the whirlwind.'[76]

For many traditional theists, such a view is somewhat akin to 'pantheism', popularised in Western culture in the thought of the 17th-century Dutch philosopher, Baruch Spinoza[77] (1632–1677) and expanded somewhat by Australian-born, Manchester-based philosopher, Samuel Alexander (1859–1938). Today, there is a range of titles: 'mystical naturalism', 'naturalistic theism', 'religious naturalism'. Echoing cell biologist Ursula Goodenough at the 2021 IRAS[78] Conference,

> A religious naturalist takes nature to mind and also takes nature to heart – seeking, and finding, deep resources in these understandings for spiritual (inward) and moral (outward) orientation, including an eco-moral orientation.[79]

In short: religious or mystical naturalism features a blending of world-views and ideas that explores trackless places and experiences which are different from most traditional expressions of religion. Deep attunement. Deep knowledge. Honouring nature all the way down.[80] Where the sacred is not a separate '*super*natural' sphere of life. More like the caffeine in coffee than like a strawberry on top of a pavlova.[81] Appreciating the sacred can be as simple as looking carefully at ordinary daily events:

- the click-clack of two branches knocking together in the wind

---

76 Atwood. *Selected Poems 1965-1975*.
77 Spinoza spoke of 'God or Nature' in such a way as to say that 'God', rightly conceived, is the same as the entire inter-connected universe.
78 Institute on Religion in an Age of Science
79 Goodenough. "Taking Nature", 2021.
80 Goodenough. "Honouring Nature", 2015.
81 Stone. *Sacred Nature*, 19.

- that rain is not a singular thing but made up of billions of individual drops of water, each with its own destination and timing
- hearing the love-making songs of the Green Grocer cicadas... all are signs enough.

★★★

The earth has now turned. The season is changing in my front garden. The skeletal branches of our Japanese Maple, triggered by warmer early-spring days and sunlight, has lured the sap within to move, to venture up, and once again engage in a new season of leaf and green-beauty creation. So spare no lament for the autumn maple leaves... 'rainbow alleluias'. Nature is never static. Life is animate, continually incarnating itself

> in microbes and maples, in humming birds and human beings... [where] we are a result of nature's inherent processes... part of the emergence of the universe itself.[82]

Nature in autumn and spring reminds us and calls us to a 'new' religious sensitivity... "The light of the eternal is in the vibrancy of the colours."[83] Thus, never let it be said that religious wisdom comes *only* from books, or 'ordained' teachers, authorised rituals, or creedal statements. Or worse, as in John Muir's case, from a tyrannical and fundamentalist father... "a narrow, angry Calvinist who tried to teach the young Muir that we are 'poor worms of the dust, conceived in sin'."[84]

Religious sensitivity *also* comes from our attentiveness, recognition and imaginative appreciation of the natural world... from sunrise to sunset. Observing the world of life around us brings many gifts as John Muir's 'spiritual pilgrimage' and 'observing' also

---

82 Bumbaugh. "Toward a Humanist Vocabulary", 2003
83 Keen. *Apology for Wonder* 210.
84 Newell. *Sacred Earth, Sacred Soul*, 149.

indicates. In what is considered by some as "big picture thinking, big-hearted love, and big screen imagination, both scientific and religious", delivered at the Millennium Peace Summit of Religious and Spiritual Leaders in August 2000, priest and storyteller Thomas Berry suggested participants go outside and look up at the sky overarching Earth and "think of the mythic foundations of our future",

> ... as we look up at the starry sky at night, and as, in the morning, we see the landscape revealed as the sun dawns over the earth – these experiences reveal a physical world but also a more profound world that cannot be bought with money, cannot be manufactured with technology, cannot be listed on the stock market, cannot be made in the chemical laboratory, cannot be reproduced with all our genetic engineering, cannot be sent by e-mail. These experiences require only that we follow the deepest feelings of the human soul.[85]

Could all this be the beginnings of a newer testament? A gospel of the natural present moment? A natural 'wild' spirituality... released from the captivity of supernatural religion? No matter how beautiful some may consider it, a supernatural worldview and the practices that reinforce it, anaesthetises us to things we need to do if we are to create sustainability for our planet, our children, and their children. "Stripped of a divine plan," suggests Canadian progressive Gretta Vosper,

> we are challenged to be active participants who can mould the world around us rather than simply passive recipients who engage, now and again, in acts of devotion with the hope of altering the course of events.[86]

---

85 Berry. "Evening Thoughts" 193-194.
86 Vosper. *Amen*, 2012.

3
A 'Wild'[87] Mysticism?
Courtship of the Particular.

> *"What we want is not permanent hibernation in some forest hut, but occasional retreat to the scenes of nature... where the thrill of being alive and of being a growing creature of earth may take hold of us and emotionalize us with the legitimate sense of creature-feeling."*
>
> Bernard Meland

A favourite quotation from one of my mentors, as already mentioned, is in an article theologian Bernard Eugene Meland (1899–1993) wrote in 1931 while still shaping his 'mystical naturalism'. "Have you ever communed in the first person with this total wealth of living life about you...?" The article's thesis was a defence of religion that in its basic form was "an appreciative reaction, or an aesthetic response, to a cosmic reality".[88]

He went on to write that if we have not stood in awe and wonder "before the unbounded totality of all reality called the universe", and begun to feel our own intimacy with all its life, then we have not experienced first-hand religion. He continued:

> Creeds and codes are not themselves religion; they are the carriers of religious experience... But woe is that life which makes these carriers his sole religious inheritance! If from those who have passed on creeds we have not acquired the eagerness to find that subtle richness in life's experience for

---

87 'Wild' is not meant in the colloquial sense of 'out of control' rather to refer to the natural, innate way the world was created: not controlled or tamed or domesticated.
88 Meland. "The Worship Mood", 665. *Unpublished Papers*, 86.

ourselves, we have received the husk, but not the grain; the symbol, but not the symbolized.[89]

So the question mark in my title 'A Wild Mysticism?' is important: a query rather than a declaration.

Sharing this journey of query are glimpses from the compelling thoughts of the 'early'[90] Bernard Meland coupled with the Celtic wisdom of philosopher, poet, Irish bard "and the splendid, searching, openly ragged-around-the-edges human being",[91] John O'Donohue (1956–2008) – both from the more 'progressive/liberal' understanding of Christianity. My journey companions will also have a fellow-traveller on a side road, Kenneth L. Patton (1911–1994). Patton, a poet, artist and respected "liberal/humanist", was the former minister of the experimental Universalist[92] Charles Street Meeting House in Boston (USA) from 1949 to the mid-1960s.[93] He developed a poetic naturalistic mysticism around the themes of 'being at-home in the universe' coupled with a 'sense of mystery' – probably sharing with Meland an influence shaped from their time at the Divinity School of the University of Chicago where there was academic 'conflict' between theism and humanism during the 1930s and 1940s. Of that conflict, professor of religious studies, Marvin Shaw, writes:

> Naturalistic theism arose within the controversy as an attempt to move beyond humanism, while accepting its naturalistic assumptions... a mediating position between classical theism and religious humanism.[94]

---

89 Meland, "The Worship Mood", 665.
90 The period 1930–1937,
91 Tippett. "Foreword", ix.
92 The Universalists and Unitarians were still courting at this time!
93 Patton's fifteen-year ministry redefined the meaning of the word Universalism by bringing the arts of all religions and cultures into 'a religion for one world.'
94 Shaw. *Nature's Grace* 17.

Seventy years ago, and many articles and Addresses later, Patton penned an essay "The Mystical Search" which included this important observation:

> Mysticism has suffered, as has religion in general, by being regarded as strictly a business by which man related himself to the supernatural world and united his being with God's. In fact, religion is so generally defined as concerned with the world beyond, that many question whether religion can be reinterpreted as moral and idealistic activity in the earthly and human realm. So with mysticism.[95]

While there are differences between Meland and O'Donohue, there are also some significant similarities.

- Both did post-graduate studies in Germany either with or on a mystic: Meland at Marburg. O'Donohue at Tubingen.
- Both have an urgent sensitivity towards humanity and our place in nature: expressed in the language of 'appreciative awareness' or 'sensitive awareness'.
- Both were "creatively out of step" with the dominate theology of their day, causing ecclesiastical superiors to become 'suspicious' of them.
- Both approached life with a well-informed, deeply rooted aesthetic, characterised by the "sensitivity of the poet."[96] To respond appreciatively to reality, to what that awareness gives. To feel at-home in the universe.

"Mysticism is not an abandonment of reason," suggested Meland, "but a new integration of emotion and reason... and not in any evangelical urge."[97] He was highly critical of supernatural religion that fostered a sense of strangeness[98] toward the natural

---

95 Patton. *Man's Hidden Search* 96-97
96 Wieman & Meland. *American Philosophies of Religion*, 292.
97 Meland. "The Mystic Returns" 157.
98 Meland. "Kinsmen of the Wild", 443.

world. Especially anthropocentrism so dissociated from nature, nature being a realm of mindless passion, impulse and mechanism.

> And though it took time to register fully, [anthropocentrism] was to mean, not only that God had created the world for man, but that God, the Creator, could best be understood in the image of man. Thus, human personality assumed absolute significance as the summit of nature and history and the apex of divinity.[99]

Similarly, but drawing inspiration from Ireland's rich spiritual heritage of Celtic thought and imagination, O'Donohue's passionate concerns were wonder, imagination, and possibility. In his second popular book, *Eternal Echoes*, he writes:

> Wonder enlarges the heart. When you wonder, you are drawn out of yourself. The cage of the ego and the railtracks of purpose no longer hold you prisoner. Wonder creates a lyrical space where thought and feeling take leave of their repetitive patterns, to regain their original impulse of reverence before the mystery of what is. Such a tiny word, yet *is* confers the highest dignity and mystery... To say something *is* means that it has real presence, it is not a fantasy nor a mere notion.[100]

Is. A puff of experience at a moment in time. A phase of process, of becoming. And that wonder, integration and sensitivity is shaped most creatively when we adopt a lifestyle that follows the advice of poets and mystics.

There is a crisis of inattention in the lives of many today. The "amusements that absorb the masses... are saddening spectacles".[101] Thus my practical thesis towards a 'wild'[102] natural mysticism: Pay

---

99 Meland. "Grace: A Dimension within Nature?" 130.
100 O'Donohue. *Eternal Echoes* 201.
101 Patton. *Man's Hidden Search*, 94.
102 'Wild' is not meant in the colloquial sense of 'out of control' rather to refer to the natural, innate way the world was created: not controlled or tamed or domesticated... (Loorz, *Church of the Wild* 6).

attention. Rejoice in it. Care for it. Cultivate a culture of reverence and gratitude. "Mysticism is the means whereby men outreach themselves", claims Patton, "extend themselves beyond previous confines, stretch the tent of their comprehension and observation to cover a larger plot of the universe".[103]

★★★

So what of mysticism? Saturated with both *super*naturalism and idealism, traditional mysticism supports the notion that knowledge of the divine "comes to one who is properly attuned, in moments of heightened awareness".[104] Early Western mysticism began to take shape around the third century and it found a special expression in medieval times with such persons as Hildegarde of Bingen (1098–1179), Meister Eckhart (original name Johannes Eckhart) (c.1260–1328), Julian of Norwich (1342–1416) and Thomas a' Kempis (1380–1471), to name but a few.

At the suggestion of his PhD supervisor, John O'Donohue studied the writings of Meister Eckhart – German Catholic theologian, philosopher, and mystic. "Meister Eckhart is for me one of the most fascinating minds of the Western tradition," wrote O'Donohue,

> a mind that had its flowering in the early part of the millennium. He was a priest, a mystic – and officially a heretic! Several people had recommended Eckhart to me over the years, and while looking around for mystical reading I stumbled on his sermons in a London bookshop... [Later] in the little town I was living in at the time, there was an antiquarian bookshop run by a cranky little man, a very conservative type. I happened to ask him one morning if he had anything on Eckhart. He disappeared upstairs and come back with

---

103 Patton. *Man's Hidden Search*, 98.
104 Meland. "Mysticism Modern", 83.

seventeen dust-covered volumes which he had had for years. It seemed providential, so I set to work on Meister Eckhart.[105]

O'Donohue suggests that Eckhart's idea of God was "that there is nothing closer to us than God. That is what made the Church suspicious of him – that Eckhart brought God too much down to earth..."[106] He explains further that the God Eckhart believed in was "an incredibly 'wild' kind of God!"

> "Wild" is something you cannot tame – and I suppose one of the things institutional religion does is to have a few 'official tamers' on hand in case the divine thing wakens up in too wild a way... Eckhart is 'wilder' in his thinking about God than even the best atheists... God is that wilderness in which everyone is alone.[107]

Eckhart's ideas became a primary and profound influence on O'Donohue in those post-doctoral years. O'Donohue claimed that Eckhart believed everything had its origin in the mind of God.

> ...people, landscapes, oceans, stars, birds, stones, flowers – none of them are here by accident but each of them was born within the mind of God... a very artistic notion of the divine imagination.[108]

The reward for Eckhart's "wild God" was to be tried before the Inquisition and condemned as a heretic! Eckhart had transgressed the traditional monotheistic tradition of transcendence or, to be more precise, vertical transcendence. Hierarchical vertical transcendence is one of the core themes of monotheistic religion.

> The direction is vertical; the ultimate and the absolute are at the top. Order triumphs over messiness, coherence

---

105 O'Donohue. *Walking in Wonder*, 29-30.
106 O'Donohue, *Walking in Wonder*, 31-32.
107 O'Donohue. *Walking in Wonder*, 34.
108 O'Donohue. *Walking in Wonder* 33.

negates confusion, beauty trumps ugliness, purpose defeats meaninglessness. As we ascend... so do we satisfy our hierarchical impulse to rise above what we were.[109]

In the vertical mode, spiritual cultivation is solitary and unrooted. One's response is made by fitting into an ideal scheme that has everything to do with "order, coherence, beauty and purpose... Gods are revealed to us who design, who have a plan, who radiate beauty and truth".[110] But there is another understanding of transcendence which certainly Meland, and perhaps O'Donohue, appears to have understood, and which Eckhart's thought may well have been exploring... At least I'd like to think Eckhart was giving it a gentle nudge! It is called horizontal transcendence, which can be described as being "about responding to the nature of nature with attunement and participation and delight." The 'delight' is with the particular: "the ladybug crawling on the rock, the fuzzy moss, the sickly dune grass, the mucky mud by the river."[111] A startling reversal of traditional theological thinking.

For we are always 'situated beings' in a particular location as there is no world posited apart from the historically ongoing one within which we find ourselves.

> Horizontal transcendence is not about hierarchy; it is about being part of the whole, being alive to all. It is infused with humility.[112]

Life becomes suddenly and marvellously abundant!

All religious orientations offer a reward. Vertical transcendence's reward is hierarchical traditions unified with a purposeful Creator. Horizontal transcendence's reward is homecoming, an attunement with nature, and our delight in participating in the great unfolding.[113]

---

109 Goodenough. "Vertical" 24.
110 Goodenough. "Vertical" 23.
111 Goodenough. "Vertical" 26.
112 Goodenough. "Vertical', 30.
113 Meland. "Religion", 69.

A 'Wild' Mysticism? Courtship of the Particular.

Victoria Loorz, author of *Church of the Wild*, writes,

> People exploit what they have merely concluded to be of value, but they defend what they love. To defend what we love we need a particularizing language, for we love what we particularly know.' This is a courtship of the particular.[114]

"Courtship of the particular" is another interesting and poetic phrase. I would place it alongside Rabbi Abraham Heschel's comment that human beings are the cantors of the universe[115] able to sing praise and thanks in the name of all the rest.

Courtship. Particular. A particular 'stone', perhaps. One from among the oldest rocks in Western Australia, that are 4.3 billion years old. Or at midsummer dawn, standing reverently at Stonehenge before the Altar Stone – a greenish-grey six-tonne sandstone block – when it is set ablaze with sunlight...

So take a stone. A 'particular' flat stone... from the island of Iona[116] in the Inner Hebrides of western Scotland, from the beach at St Columba's Bay and catch its checkered colours. Or another stone – the gift between a Gentoo penguin to another during 'courting'...

> Hurtling through space in some asteroid belt when earth got in the way.
> Here long before we were ever dreamed.
> Holding out against transience.
> Always faithfully there.
> Perfectly silent.[117]

---

114 Loorz. *Church of the Wild*, 128.
115 See https://www.hebrewcollege.edu/wp-content/uploads/2018/11/Heschel-The-Vocation-of-the-Cantor.pdf
116 Iona, on the Atlantic edge of British Isles and the sixth-century birthplace of Scottish Christianity, is a place of international pilgrimage.
117 This section is indebted to O'Donohue reflections in *Four Elements*.

"Some of the oldest rocks in the world are on the western side of the island of Iona in Scotland," writes John O'Donohue in his reflection 'Stone and Fire'. Because these rocks

> remember and preserve in their clear interiority the primal silence from an aeon before life risked itself into texture, before individuality ever discovered its inner mirror.[118]

★★★

At-homeness in the universe... said Meland back then, ahead of his time. Some forty-five years later, he added a cautionary lament. At-homeness entails that we understand ourselves

> not as plunderers and exploiters of nature's resources, but as creatures of earth, born of its processes, nurtured and sustained by the subtle and intricate inter-change as humanly evolved organisms within this enveloping atmosphere... I cringed at the thought the Christian legacy setting its seal of approval upon it, either through glib, biblical utterances, or through intricate arguments offered by theologians whose views of man and creation hardly entitled them to be called a child of earth. And I hoped that God might find their views offensive, too.[119]

Courtship of the particular...

> Pay attention!
> Rejoice in it!
> Care for it!
> Cultivate a culture of reverence and gratitude!

We need to unearth our 'wild' roots!

Nature (with or without the god G-o-d[120]) is so significant now in the twenty-first century, that all our beliefs must be reformulated so as to take nature into account. As such, this will require us to

---

118 O'Donohue. *Four Elements*, 148.
119 Meland. "Grace: A Dimension within Nature?", 135.
120 I use this expression in order to emphasise that the god G-o-d is not an identifiable thing "over there."

abandon our primary understanding of Earth as a natural resource for unlimited human use and to cultivate a primary understanding of Earth

> as the source whence we were born, the nourishment that sustains us while we are living, our healing in moments of distress, and the way to our final destiny.[121]

Theistic persons traditionally offer reverence to a *super*natural deity, as Kenneth Patton pointed out in his comment above. Theistic naturalists conceive of G-o-d as the creative process within the universe. Non-theistic persons are called to revere the whole enterprise of planetary existence, for without reverence we will gradually descend into ecocide.[122] Whatever else scientific thinking has contributed, it has certainly amplified the activity and scope of the natural world, away from the *super*natural to the natural. Taking nature to heart, suggests philosopher Jerome Stone, "does not leave a person with any fewer spiritual benefits than taking to heart the teachings of *super*naturalist traditions".[123]

We don't need to look for rarified supernatural revelation. We simply need to recognise the sacrality of everything around us. And that recognition needs the language of reverence that conveys the depth, richness and complexity of our natural world and voices that call for faithfulness to the richness of that lived experience instead of abstractions about nature.[124] "There is only one world, that of nature, in which all things belong... The mystery is not *in* the flower; the flower *is* the mystery. All things are the mystery. They are. That is all."[125]

Thus the most imperative undertaking in life – call it one's religion or philosophy of life – is the endeavour to adapt oneself

---

121 Berry. *Sacred Universe*, 168.
122 London, "Renewing Our Sense of Wonder" Interview. Also Brussatt, Interview.
123 Stone. *Sacred Nature*, 116.
124 Inbody. *Constructive Theology*, 233.
125 Patton. *Man's Hidden Search*, 93.

courageously to the facts of existence and thus prepare to live the life of integrity.[126]

A wild mysticism? My query raises its head again. Not in the occult, misty sense, but in the sense that it claims the roots of human life go into the universe itself.

>   Practise noticing and listening.
>   Inhale and absorb nature's elixir.
>   Make nature central to any belief system.
>   Follow the rhythm of nature through the seasons.
>   Be open to journeying in trackless 'heretical' places.

All these being the groundwork of a mystical naturalism and the basis for a new theistic mood!

We are the earth speaking to the earth. Because we can only grow into an authentic life with integrity by being immersed in the natural world, out of which we were 'begotten' in the first place as earthlings "and not merely ensouled beings awaiting our fuller realisation in a life hereafter."[127]

A 'wild' mysticism!

>   Surplusage of mystery in life.[128]
>   Full-orbed natural universe.

If we are to find the mysticism of natural experience, we must attend to nature in its particularity.

>   A mossy stone pitted by wind and rain.
>   A tree alive in its soil.
>   A ladybug on an autumn leaf.
>   Standing on a beach being soaked slowly by a shower
>   of rain as it moves in from the ocean.

---

126 Meland. *Modern Man's Worship*, 254
127 O'Murchu. *Ecological Spirituality*, 176.
128 Meland. "Religion", 69.

Experiences *of*, *in* and *as* nature. Life becomes loveless and drab when shorn of its stars and dandelions! Because being at-home in the universe, soaking in the brilliant flourishing around oneself, both intellectually and emotionally, is a precondition not merely for survival but for the articulation and development of our deeper selves, as earthlings.

> The natural mystic acknowledges the earthly nature of his reactions. He is not afraid of his body and its feelings, revelling in the sights, sounds, colors, tastes, smells, textures of the world. They are all grist of his mystic mill.[129]

★★★

So some last words at the start of a new beginning already begun: a 'wild' mystical naturalism which begins with a courtship of the particular.

Bernard Meland

> – The naturalistic mystic, like other aesthetic naturalists, approaches life with the sensitivity of the poet. His mystical experience is akin to the experience of the poet, the artist, or the lover of nature: charged with a profound fullness, evocative of great emotion and feeling. It is profound and full and stirring because of the dimension of its grasp, not because of any occult feeling that accompanies the envisagement. Like the poet he includes immense ranges in his grasp. He envisages reality in synthesis.[130]

John O'Donohue

> – The imagination is the great friend of possibility. Where the imagination is awake and alive, fact never hardens or closes but remains open, inviting you to new thresholds of possibility and creativity.[131]

---

129 Patton. *Man's Hidden Search*, 115.
130 Wieman & Meland. *American Philosophies of Religion*, 292.
131 O'Donohue. *Anam Cara*, 183.

Kenneth Patton
— There can be no separation between natural and religious mysticism. The experience of nature and human nature is religious experience.[132]

---

132 Patton. *Man's Hidden Search*, 117.

4

Hyacinths, Biscuits... and the Fragrance of Life

*"To feel religiously is to speak with the tongues of poets...
Like the language of art, poetry and friendship, the language of religion
is suggestive, not descriptive or definitive."*

Bernard Meland

Carl Sandburg (1878–1967), the widely regarded American poet, author, Chicago journalist, and three-times Pulitzer Prize winner – twice for poetry – once defined poetry as 'the synthesis of hyacinths and biscuits'. Intrigued, I began to search for its context.

Now I didn't discover where he actually placed the comment – in a poem, that is – but I did find where hundreds of others have quoted it. So I am prepared to accept it as a genuine Sandburg saying. By-the-way, of poetry Sandburg also wrote nearly 40 other so-called 'definitions'. Some of those are:

> Poetry is a phantom script telling how rainbows are made and why they go away.
> Poetry is an echo, asking a shadow to dance.
> Poetry is the opening and closing of a door, leaving those who look through to guess about what is seen during the moment.

It wasn't until I read the comments of another poet – who also wrestled with his 'hyacinths/biscuits' definition – that I reckoned I began to appreciate some of the meanings attributed to it that made it so attractive to many. 'The putting together of unlike things to give us a new view of our world'.[133] A 'synthesis' view of life.

***

As it happens, Bernard Meland (1899–1993) said of Sandburg's poetry comment that it also defines life, "for life, too, is a synthesis of biscuits and hyacinths."[134] Nearly 90 years ago, Meland wrote

> The biscuits are the mills that grind the wheat into flour; they are the train wheels that carry the flour to the bakeries; and the wagons that deliver the loaves to the grocer, and to hungry humanity. Biscuits are the rugged, commonplace essentials of life. They are the whole wheat of life. Hyacinths, on the other hand, represent the loveliness of life. They grace the garden walls. They breathe fragrance into the world. They send the chills up and down one's spine, and evoke the "Ohs!" and "Ahs!" Hyacinths create our precious memories: a baby's smile, the lover's caress, the parent's fondness for his child. Hyacinths are the glorious, stirring ecstasies of a buoyant heart. They bloom on a clear, cold, moonlight night, and they blend their color with the calm, quiet sunset. Hyacinths are all those many things and experiences which enhance life with mystery, color and fragrance.[135]

Meland goes on to say,

> All that we do, and everything we handle, combines these two sides of life, for it is the nature of nature to synthesise biscuits and hyacinths... The one suggests relative value in the sense of being a means toward an end; the other suggests intrinsic value in the sense of being, itself, an end.[136]

---

133 Monahan. "Bite into Poetry"
134 Meland. *Modern Man's Worship*, 279. Meland changed the order).
135 Meland. *Modern Man's Worship* 279.
136 Meland. *Modern Man's Worship* 279-280.

The two sides of life are commonly called the 'practical' or 'instrumental' and the 'aesthetic' or 'intrinsic'. Western society has always placed more value on the 'practical' rather than the 'aesthetic'. Perhaps this is why he 'who is currently (2021) moonlighting as our prime minister', gave a financial handout to sales people and bar staff during the 2020 Covid lockdowns, but not to the arts – dancers, musicians, poets!

In traditional religion, the 'two sides' are often represented as: 'Doing the will of G-o-d' verses 'Be still, and know that I am G-o-d'. This difference in religious sensibilities has been an important factor throughout history the world over. But in reality the aesthetic and the practical are two sides of the one world. "Our environment," writes Meland again, "is vaster and richer at any one moment than we ever consciously recognize during working hours when utility is in the saddle."[137] So what does 'being aesthetic' mean? Again the wisdom of Meland:

> Being aesthetic means reaching out beyond the obvious and the useful to this vaster and richer content that environs us. This aspect is the opposite of standardization. It tends toward innovation. It cultivates spontaneity, originality, deep insight, and broad sympathy. It gives dimension and intensity to life. The only way to achieve this aesthetic measure of life is by frequently exposing one-self to the awesome, the mystifying, and the inspiring. Live in the presence of that which gives altitude to emotions. Enter frequently into deepening contact with the wide cosmic expanse of life. Turn from the critical mood occasionally to see life in synthesis. See the world synthesized in a flower, a sea, or in a human being. Catch glimpses of the whole of reality. Contemplate your own life blended with the total movement of life. Envisaging these wider reaches of reality not only enlarges the scope of living, but it sensitizes our feel for life and beautifies its quality.[138]

---

[137] Meland. *Modern Man's Worship* 288.
[138] Meland. *Modern Man's Worship*, 288.

Or, catch the wisdom of poet Mary Oliver (1935–2019) – another Pulitzer Prize winner. A strong sense of place, and of identity in relation to it, is central to her poetry. Her creativity was stirred by the *actuality* of nature[139] – to look candidly at the world – and her poems are filled with imagery from daily walks: shore birds, water snakes, the phases of the moon, and humpback whales. "Just pay attention to the natural world around you – the goldfinches, the swan, the wild geese. They will tell you what you need to know."[140]

When reviewing Oliver's work, one literary critic wrote: 'Her poems are firmly located in the places where she has lived or traveled... her moments of transcendence arise organically from the realities of swamp, pond, woods and shore.' While another commented: 'At its most intense, her poetry aims to peer beneath the constructions of culture and reason that burden us with an alienated consciousness to celebrate the primitive, mystical visions of the natural world.'

Pay attention! Experience! Imagine! Such attention and experience comes from being immersed in what is, and seeing the overlooked. As another has said: we are cosmic and we are local.[141] The natural world is all around us, and we are an integral part of it. Appreciation of the benefits of nature – of being at-home in the universe and the environment in which we must fulfil our lives – is an ancient wisdom we are only barely beginning to regain, as the Earth heats, glaciers melt, rainforests are logged, and species vanish.

At times, we seek to *critically understand* and to use those environing realities. Thus a poetic response is often the most appropriate and shrewdest analyst of social concerns including frustrated hopes and political skulduggery. But at other times we will respond *appreciatively* to the deep significance of these

---

139 Meland would claim 'therein lies the religious quality of its mood – its actuality'. "Kinsmen of the Wild", 443.
140 Franklin. "Mary Oliver's Critics", (2017)
141 Fleischman. *Wonder*, 165.

environings. As I have stated on other occasions: we need both the voice of the rational – to keep any community free from sloppy sentimentality – as well as the concern of the creative artist – the rich, deep, not entirely rational forms of expression shaped by metaphor, the poetic, myth and parable – to strike a chord and resonate within.

But it is at the level of the imagination that any full engagement with life takes place. What is now required is a different religious sensitivity: a natural spirituality or an ecological spirituality. Because nature is the thread that completes the tapestry of life.[142] "Whether or not we believe that there is something more", writes Philip Hefner (1932–2024), "nature is so significant that all our beliefs must be reformulated so as to take nature into account."[143]

Religion is born out of the sense of wonder and awe of the majesty and fearsomeness of the universe itself.[144] But religion is also poetry – at least according to 'geologian', Thomas Berry (1914–2009). In an interview with Australian church historian and former priest, Paul Collins, Berry claimed:

> Religion is poetry or it is nothing! How can a person be religious without being poetic? Certainly God is a poet; it is God who made rainbows, butterflies and flowers. It is the most absurd thing in the world to think of dealing with religion in any other way than poetry or music... You cannot do it any other way.[145]

But then Collins went on to add:

> Deprived of nature with its beauty, multiplicity, mystery, complexity and otherness, our imaginations would shrivel up,

---

142 A 'theory of naturalised spirituality' can be found in Jerome Stone. *Sacred Nature*, 76-80.
143 Hefner. "Forward", x.
144 Berry. *Selected Writings*, 74.
145 Collins. *ABC*, 2010

and we would lose our ability to perceive and experience the deeper feelings and intuitions that give real meaning to our lives. For nature is the source of our origin and the context of our continuing evolution and spiritual development. Without imagination we would lose all sense of ourselves as human beings.

Life glows on! Such is the poetics of life. All those many things and experiences which enhance life with mystery, colour, and fragrance. Biscuits and hyacinths included!

> As we consider this Earth,
> our home,
> and we, our presence upon it,
> may we be moved to see ourselves
> as particles of the whole
> and walk in reverence.[146]

---

146 Vosper. *We All Breath*, 32.

5

Festivals, Transience... and Leaves

"Our origins are of the earth... so there is in us a deeply seated response to the natural universe, which is part of our humanity."
Rachel Carson

One of the amazing things about the human mind is the recognition that time passes. Holidays, festivals and celebrations chronicle human history. Past and present. We are the creatures who celebrate. We dance, sing, tell stories, feast, fast and dramatise important moments and events in our lives. Life refuses to be embalmed alive!

We are part of the growing cycle of the planet, as we are nourished by the elements, by vegetation and animal life, and at the end of our cycle, in turn providing nourishment for those same elements, vegetation and animal life.

The way in which we observe and celebrate the unfolding year is very important to our day life. This is especially true when the majority of us live in an urban environment where the seasonal shifts are less readily perceptible, where the growth cycle which annually unfolds is much easier to ignore. As human beings, we are also part of the growth cycle of the planet, being nourished by the elements, by vegetation and animal life and, at the end of our cycle, in turn providing nourishment for those same elements, vegetation and animal life. As year succeeds year, each season provides new lessons, insights and opportunities for us to understand our role in the planetary web of life.[147]

---

[147] Matthews. *Celtic Book of Days* 6.

Humans and the universe were made for each other. Priest and 'geologian' Thomas Berry (1914–2009) suggested:

> Our experience of the universe finds festive expression in the great moments of seasonal transformation, such as the dark of winter, the exuberance of springtime, the warmth and brightness of summer, the lush abundance of autumn. These are the ever-renewing moments of celebration of the universe, moments when the universe is in some depth of communion with itself in the intimacy of all its components.[148]

The interdependence of humans and the earth comes into clear focus in the changing of the seasons. Traditional festivals have ancient roots springing from very early ideas of life, the world and the heavens. Most annual Autumn celebrations, for instance, originated from seasonal changes in the lives of agricultural people. These festivals are usually related to the movement of the earth, the sun or the moon, "and the changes these movements made in the lives of human beings whose behaviour was said to be governed by them."[149] But up until modern times it was the Christian church that was seen to be the official promoter and guardian of our festivals. "Unfortunately," writes New Zealand theologian, Sir Lloyd Geering

> because [the church] became increasingly divorced from the natural world and interpreted human life in other-worldly terms, it now has a great deal of unlearning to do before it can give to our ecological age the spiritual guidance that is so badly needed.[150]

Scientists no longer describe the world as a fertile blend of the four elements: earth, wind, fire and water. They talk *wonder*-fully about electrons, protons and neutrons. (And sometimes about

---

148 Tucker & Grim. *Thomas Berry* 179.
149 Nickerson. *Celebrate the Sun*, x.
150 Geering. *The Greening of Christianity*, 50.

Festivals, Transience... and Leaves

morons!) But the four elements remain the entrance to our common experiences of the 'web' we call 'nature' and 'natural'. For we are thoroughly nature. To claim otherwise is to attempt to place human beings and everything we do in some rare unimaginable realm beyond the universe, thus rendering the power of our origins lost and our obligations vague.

Today, in the month called March named after the Roman god of war, and included in both the Julian and Gregorian calendars, we who live in the southern hemisphere are well into celebrating Autumn, called the season of thanksgiving, harvest... and leaves. Sandwiched between blazing Summer and chilly Winter, Autumn is the cooling off season. The 'Season of mists and mellow fruitfulness', according to the poet Keats. The duration of daylight becomes noticeably shorter. Night-time arrives earlier. Temperatures begin to drop considerably. Most vegetative growth decreases, although as Albert Camus (1913–1960) wrote: *Autumn is a second spring when every leaf is a flower.*

In Autumn, the season of unavoidable endings, the shedding of leaves from deciduous trees is a significant feature. Millions of monarch butterflies travel thousands of miles across North America to arrive in the mountainous region of Mexico, where they remain until spring. Not to be outdone, we on the NSW Central Coast had a unique event in 2020 when thousands of white butterflies used a mate's back yard as a resting place. He writes:

> Last Sunday I woke from an afternoon nap around 3.00pm and thought I was still dreaming. Out the back window I saw a continuous flow of white butterflies. Hundreds of them. They were on a mission as they were not flitting around but flying straight from the south to the north along the creek at the back of our house. You could see many in the front of the house too but not quite as thick and the trees at the back made a darker background. I had never seen anything like it

before. The flight went on for hours, even the next morning there were some but the numbers were dwindling of course.[151]

What was happening was a Caper White Butterfly[152] migration. A rare phenomenon that only happens every six to ten years, usually in Spring. The butterflies maintain flight around 2-3m above the ground during the day.

★★★

I particularly like Autumn. It is a season of transition and it can be spectacular. I especially liked Autumn when we lived in Canberra... A 'native bush' capital yes, but also a capital full of northern deciduous trees. Yellow. Brown. Red. Burgundy. Autumn's technicoloured biology. Rainbow alleluias. The leaves we see in Spring and Summer are green because of chlorophyll, that miracle of evolution whereby plants convert sunlight, oxygen and water into energy. The leaves we see in Autumn, again a result of evolution, is chlorophyll receding as the leaves and plants 'energy engines' shut down. This allows the colours from other chemicals to show their yellow and orange hues... and finally fall.

But this is not trees recycling. Again, according to evolution, what they do is to make their leaves in such a way that the bacteria in the soil do the recycling for them. Presto! Next Spring's fertiliser. In sync with nature. Not working against nature. As Autumn turns into Winter, the Canberra landscape changes. Barren grey sentinels stand among their evergreen siblings. And not a politician in sight!

Trees have always fascinated me. Right from the time as a young boy I learnt to climb some of their more juvenile and smaller

---

151 Peter Lambert. Personal correspondence.
152 Quoting from the website of Butterfly Conservation South Australia Inc. "This butterfly (*Belenois aurota*) has its [evolutionary] origins in Africa where a large number of morphologically similar species occur. ... historically made its way to India, and from there probably ... via Indonesia to Australia where it is now represented by *B. java*."

offspring on our annual camping adventures to The Grampians (*Gariwerd*) in country Victoria. Not to mention conquering dad's apricot tree, and its fruit, down at the wood-heap!

Do you know, for example, that trees can communicate with each other through their roots, even when they are many kilometres apart? Or that they are nothing but flirts? The scents and blossoms of fruit trees and willows are billboards to draw attention to themselves and invite passing bees to sate themselves. Sweet nectar is the reward the insects get in exchange for the incidental dusting they receive while they visit.

Each is the natural world making its own rules and its own intricate webs – ecosystems – of energy. After all, trees are important to our lives in many ways. The most obvious is their role in producing the oxygen we breathe and sequestering carbon dioxide to help protect our atmosphere.

Over the course of their lives [trees] store up to 22 tons of carbon dioxide in their trunks, branches, and root systems... The forest is really a gigantic carbon dioxide vacuum that constantly filters out and stores this component of the air.[153]

Deep in the bush – wetland or state forest – surrounded by big old trees I am often stuck by three important ingredients in nature: awe, wonder, and curiosity. That feeling of being in the presence of something vast that transcends one's understanding of the world. Experiencing.

Likewise, "[t]his is a library built by many hands," Scottish artist and founder Katie Peterson said at the 2024 festival of the Future Library in Nordmarka, Norway – a forest of books established in 2014, that will grow, unread, for a hundred years. Explaining the Future Library, David Farrier writes:

> Every year a writer contributes a text – a story, a poem, even a novel, there is no limit – that will be held in trust until 2114,

---

153 Wohlleben. *Hidden Life of Trees* 93

when an anthology of the work will be printed on paper from trees specially planted in Nordmarka, a vast forest of pine, spruce, and birch outside Oslo. Each new deposit is marked by a summer handover ceremony in the grove.

His explanation continued...

> A library can coordinate our time with that of future generations, with a forest clock we can synchronise with an entire ecosystem, calibrating our tempo with nature's intricate groove. In coordinating with wild clocks and composing new rituals, we might also redesign the systems and infrastructures that sustain modern life.[154]

As each new writer hands over their work, it causes one to wonder what message they had left for the next century and what it felt like to assume that responsibility. Wonder. Curiosity. Awe.

★★★

The seasons invite us to look for more daily experiences of awe. And what the science of awe suggests is that opportunities for awe surround us, and their benefits are profound.

> ... you don't have to do extravagant, extraordinary experiences in nature to feel awe or to get benefits. By taking a few minutes to enjoy flowers that are blooming or a sunset in your day-to-day life, you also improve your well-being.[155]

Awe is inspired by something larger than one's self or experience, and that encounter helps expand our understanding of the world... to transcend science as mere fact, and to find renewed excitement in living. And it is driven by a sense of curiosity.

We are the species that sees but doesn't only instinctively respond to what we see; we internalise it, engage with it emotionally,

---

154 Farrier. "Wild Clocks", 2025.
155 Craig Anderson quoted in Suttie, "Why is Nature...", 2019.

and try to find meaning in the moment. We experience life in a many-dimensional manifold that blends perception with a multicolored subjective response. And we love the way this richness of the now makes us feel, even if we have no clue how it all happens.[156]

The world is luminous. It is a richness of colour, form, atmosphere, of relationships, contrasts, and suggested meanings, no matter what kind of day or the season.[157] To nurture the joy of wonder is to be attuned to the simple beauty of the unexpected. It may reveal itself in the silence of an old dark forest, or in that strange uncomfortable warmth we feel "when we witness something that defies rational explanation."[158] Explorers, artists, poets, and scientists know of such wonder. So can we in Autumn. Especially in watching gold and red autumn leaves pirouette to the ground in a light wind. New Zealand theologian and hymn writer, William L. Wallace's (1933–2024) poem 'The Cycles of Nature' begins to touch on the delight in seasons:

> Interwoven web of life
> holding as one
> stream and song,
> sinew and silence,
> seedtime and harvest,
>   how I delight in you
>   and you in me...[159]

Likewise Mary Acherson's "Summer Is Here"...

> Summer is here – lush, seductive...
> Sultry breezes awaken memories of summers past,
> lure us to beaches, decks... ice cream.

---

156 Gleiser. "Wonder", 2019.
157 Patton. *Man's Hidden Search* 70.
158 Gleiser. "Wonder", 2019.
159 Wallace. "The Cycles of Nature" in *Harvest for the World*, 174.

> Our senses are aroused by abundant life – verdant full trees,
> nighttime cricket lullabies that fade to morning wake-up birdcalls.
> Buzzing, hovering insects startle and harass on afternoon walks...[160]

Or by Mary Gergen's springtime "Be Praised by Butterfly":

> Be praised, my God, by butterfly and dragonfly wings exercising for their first flight.
> Be praised by lightning and thunder causing spring showers.
> Be praised by the silent voice of grass growing and trees budding...[161]

Autumn is a season of great beauty, but it is also a season of decline: the days grow shorter, the light is suffused, and summer's abundance decays toward winter's death. Faced with this inevitable winter, what does nature do in autumn? John Palka says: She scatters the seeds that will bring new growth in the spring. She scatters them with amazing abandon. And as neuroscientist John Palka continues: This hopeful notion that living is hidden within dying is surely enhanced by the visual glories of autumn. What artist would ever have painted a season of dying with such a vivid palette if nature had not done it first. "Here's the thing," adds professor of astrophysics, Adam Frank,

> we're on the planet for about 100 years if we are really lucky. Then we die and who knows what happens? Given that inescapable fact, you'd think we might spend more time being amazed at everything – the trees, the birds, the rocks, the sky.

---

160 Acherson's "Summer Is Here" SBNR.Org. August 2009.
161 Goergen. "Be Praised by Butterfly". *Earth Prayers*, 299.

Festivals, Transience... and Leaves

All that beautiful amazing stuff is just here, working pretty well on its own. That should be cause enough for wonder.[162]

And a simple celtic 'blessing' from Caitlin Matthews:

> May the year turn blessedly for you,
> and may the gates of the year reveal new treasures
> in every season of your life![163]

We stand in awe of the *mysterious tremendous*, the great mystery.

---

162 Frank. "Whither...", 2019.
163 Matthews. *Celtic Book of Days*, 9.

6

Remembering We Too are Desert Flowers

"The desert is beautiful because it hides, somewhere, a garden."
Rubem Alves

This week saw the commencement of the traditional religious season called Lent. It began a few days ago... on Wednesday 14 February. The day was also St Valentine's Day.

Traditionally... well, in 18th-century England, St Valentine's Day evolved into an occasion in which lovers expressed their love for each other by presenting flowers, offering confectionery, and sending greeting cards.

Traditionally... well, since the year 1000CE, Ash Wednesday got its name from the act of being marked with ashes – previous year's burnt palm branches – when worshippers gather and are reminded of their sinfulness and mortality. Mmm. Love and sin. All on the same day!

Lent is associated with the story of the Jewish Galilean sage called Yeshu'a/Jesus, and his 40-day stay or testing into the desert wilderness. The story says it happened at the beginning of his brief public activity in the north-west corner of the Galilee, in the early Roman Empire, sometime between the years 26-36CE.

So, let me share a few cameos reflecting on 'desert', 'Lent' and a bit of 'progressive' theology to boot!

★★★

Perhaps the two most forbidding landscapes on Earth are (i) the frozen, volcanic desert at the intersection of Chile, Bolivia and

Argentina – "a splashy, chaotic kaleidoscope of white and blue ice, indigo water, gold and yellow sand, black and red lava..."; and (ii) the area around Lake Disappointment in the Gibson Desert of Australia – "like an inspired abstract impressionist painting, ragged brushstrokes scattered over a dappled ground, colours and shapes too many and too amorphous to name..."[164]

Australia is an ancient and distinctive land, with animals and plant life that are quite remarkable in their own right. It also has ten named deserts, the largest being the Great Victoria Desert which crosses the border into both Western Australia and South Australia. It is over 800 kilometres wide and covers an area of 348,750 square kilometres. In total, the ten deserts cover nearly 1.4 million square kilometres or 18% of the Australian mainland. However, approximately 35% of the Australian continent receives so little rain it is effectively desert. Result? Australia has been called the driest continent on earth. Some of this 'desert' experience I know first-hand, especially the distracting lure of the shimmering mirage, having been brought up in the dry Wimmera/Mallee area of Victoria and journeyed many times into the Little Desert!

> "The parched earth cracks and groans
> under the blazing sun across the wide land..." (*Dorothy McRae-McMahon*)

In the mid-1800s, when the European explorers – perhaps the most famous were Irish-born police inspector Robert O'Hara Burke and surveyor and meteorologist William John Wills – set out to cross the harsh Australian continent, they, and their sponsors, hoped to find a large inland sea

> set within a fertile wilderness that needed only the agricultural hand of civilised man to be brought into full potential as a land of plenty. With dismay they learned that the lakes

---

164 Campbell. *Face of the Earth*, 291.

were ephemeral at best, the soils were not fertile, rain was unpredictable, rivers flowed inland when they flowed at all, and life followed a boom-and-bust pattern. They called this 'empty' land the 'dead center' and started filling it with cattle.[165]

The perception of what is a desert, wilderness area, varies greatly. It depends on the different exposures people have to nature and the 'great outdoors'. To a person living on the coast, the desert is often dry and arid and dusty. A place without life. Stones and boulders. The Uluru-Kata Tjuta National Park in central Australia is the most well-known desert area. However, for desert dwellers in Australia's 'outback', beyond Charleville, Coober Pedy, Lightning Ridge and Kalgoorlie, it has a compelling fascination, as a place vibrant with life.

The spinifex-hummocks are blue grey with amber glints. They look soft but they are prickly and hard. They survive tenaciously because no grazing animal can eat them out or destroy their roots. It may look as if nothing can live in the desert, but underneath the spinifex, the desert creatures leave their tracks in the red sand. No life stirs all day, but come night... lizards, mice, bats and the rare animals of the desert live their delicate but vastly tough lives in this harsh habitat.

A little closer to home, some historians claim that for the first white settlers in New South Wales the landscape seemed barren, uninhabited, desolate - even hostile. Because it lacked the plants and animals of Europe. According to historian Grace Karskens, the Sydney wilderness environment was described as both 'very romantic, beautifully formed by nature' as well as 'the worst country in the world': "... an 'alien landscape', where nature was 'upside down' and flora and fauna were so unnervingly weird".

Why such contradiction? Conditions for the convicts and early settlers were harsh, undeniably primitive, and uncomfortable.

---

165 Campbell. *Face of the Earth*, 220.

Farming was pre-basic and the farmers lived in poverty. The drive to clear the dense bushland of the ever-creeping vegetation, and establish public farms, was to establish the initial food supply for the prison colony. Such conditions were also presented and remembered as places of torment and brutality...

> an awful over-sea gaol, offering no prospect of advancement or liberation, where the will of the prisoner turnkey was law, where death was the punishment for the most trifling crimes, and a reproachful look was punished with the lash.[166]

★★★

Now to connect some of this with a brief suggestion and then a short aphorism. The suggestion... Lent, yes for 'progressives', is a very real time where many can once again, in an intentional way, seek out the presentness of the sacred lurking in the most unlikely of places, waiting to be uncovered, found and embraced. If we only see the desert as a place of harsh, relentlessness... where people face despair and animals die of thirst, the desert experience will always be an alien danger.

So too our 'desert' and 'autumn days'...

> So much of what I'd do I can't.
> I've grown accepting of the fact.
> The very young claim it's growing old.
> I say it's growing up.
> If not, let them play Joshua and stop the sun.
> They'll learn soon enough.
> As for me, I'll go with time...
> I have, yet, a while, and things to be, and much to do.[167]

Now the aphorism... A Zen teacher said to his students:

---

166 Karskens. *Colony* 94 (Conditions at Toongabbie).
167 Coots. *Seasons of the Self* 50, 63.

> If you raise a speck of dust, the nation flourishes,
>   but the elders furrow their brows.
> If you don't raise a speck of dust, the nation perishes,
>   but the elders relax their brows.

If we listen to cosmologists, they say we are made from dust – essentially stardust. We are all connected – biologically and spiritually – with planet Earth and with all its 'other than human' beings. Echoing the words of William Blake (1757-1827), former professor of biology at the University of Washington, John Palka, suggests:

> To see a world in a grain of sand – to peer so deeply into the nature of any one thing that the riches of the Universe begin to be revealed – that to me is the essence of science as a quest. Not as a profession or a career, not as a niche in complex modern society, but as a quest for understanding one's deepest nature.[168]

Our Zen teacher probably had a different thought in mind. To raise a speck of dust is to stir up goodness, struggle for justice, speak up for those who stutter or do not speak the languages of power, band together to stand resolutely and non-violently before evil and refuse to be absorbed into it or intimidated by it.

For many traditional Christians, Lent is a time of sorry self-deprecation. I, and many others, are not helped by that perspective. From a progressive perspective, Lent can be a time when, in positive and intentional ways, our focused actions can enable others to flourish. When our selfless actions seep into the world 'like the scent of perfume distilled in the air'... encouraging and giving fresh heart to those around us, and strengthening the bonds of community.

Judging from what little firm knowledge we have of Jesus, he is remembered as undermining popular religious wisdom, forcing

---

[168] John Palka. *Nature's Depths*, web site, 15/11/2015.

his hearers to take a second look at the traditions that helped them make their way in the world. And he was able, with a storyteller's imagination, to set people free from images and ideas and religious practices that bound them into fear, and a false sense of separation from the spirit of all life.

None of this makes him *super*natural. Or divine. Or No. 2 in the Trinity. Just human. Catholic feminist theologian, Elizabeth Johnson, noted for publishing books that appear to 'strain relations between the church hierarchy and Catholic theologians', writes:

> Born of a woman… and the Hebrew gene pool, [he] was a creature of earth, a complex unit of minerals and fluids, an item in the carbon, oxygen, and nitrogen cycles, a moment in the biological evolution of this planet. Like all human beings, he carried within himself the signature of the supernovas and the geology and life history of the Earth…[169]

Whatever conclusion one might end up with about him, it must be a possible Jesus and not an incredible one. And a possible Jesus, according to theologian David Galston, is a Jesus situated in his historical circumstances

> and who did things and said things that a real person could have reasonably believed or done at that time. An incredible Jesus is the one who came from the sky, who performed miracles by fiat, and who was as dead as a doornail only to magically return to life.[170]

Some ten years later, Galston issued this lament:

> The shock value of the historical Jesus, regardless of how one approaches the question, lies in the simple truth that Jesus was a human being like anyone. The Jesus of history does not hold the confessed Son of God status that Christianity has given him. He was, like all of us, a human being who was

---

169 Johnson. "Deep Incarnation".
170 Galston. *Embracing the Human Jesus*, 50.

right sometimes and wrong at other times. Giving back to Jesus his humanity requires, on the part of later generations like us, a certain act of generosity and, even, humility toward him. Accepting Jesus as a human being, not a Savior or a God, is the sincere act of loving him both as he was and for who he was. People who hold this respectful quality of love for Jesus are, amazingly, not welcome in the church.[171]

★★★

The desert is a place where one does not expect to find life. A god-forsaken place we might say. Historically, settlement for most 'latecomers' in Australia has been at the edge, by the sea – on a large island. If Aboriginal people are a land-dreaming people, we latecomers are a sea-dreaming people. Such a sentiment is endorsed by author, Tim Winton:

> The desert is a spiritual place, but we are coastal people, a people who predominantly dwell on our continent's edge. It is there on the beach or pretty near it that the majority of Australians have discovered many things about life and what it means deep down to be Australian...[172]

This Lent, in the wilderness of our 21st century cities, furrowed by freeways and shaded by skyscrapers rather than demoralising gibber plains and ridge after ridge of red sand, may we remember that in our dry 'autumn' seasons we, too, are tiny seeds, at rest and waiting, dormant yet undefeated. Desert flowers. Endless wonder.

---

171 Galston. "The Historical Jesus is not the Christ" (2023).
172 Winton, *The Land's Edge*, 36-37.

7

The Landscape is...

"We are locked in a dance with landscapes, moulding the contours as they shape our souls."
Andrew Leigh

Indigenous Peoples around the world have three common characteristics that are all intimately connected: (i) they have an intimate, conscious relationship with their place; (ii) they are stable 'sustainable' cultures, often lasting for thousands of years, and (iii) they have a rich ceremonial and ritual life.

By contrast, Western industrial/techno culture has tried to relate to the world around us primarily through the rational, left side of our brain. We have tended to idolise ideals, reason, and logic. As a result, suggests 'deep ecologist' Dolores LaChapelle, we are failing. "If we are to re-establish a viable relationship," she urges,

> we will need to rediscover the wisdom of these other cultures who knew that their relationship to the land and to the natural world required the whole of their being.[173]

★★★

More than two centuries ago, the English poet, painter and printmaker William Blake (1757–1827) wrote four of the most often quoted lines in English literature... They are the opening lines of his 1803 poem *Auguries of Innocence*:

To see a world in a grain of sand / And a heaven in a wild flower / Hold infinity in the palm of your hand / And eternity in an hour...

---

[173] LaChapelle. "Ritual is Essential" (1984).

As many a naturalist and biologist has claimed, with Blake, to indeed see a world in a grain of sand,

> to peer so deeply into the nature of any one thing that the riches of the Universe begin to be revealed – that is the essence of science as a quest… for understanding one's deepest nature.[174]

The beginning of developing an environmental consciousness… Envisaging these wider reaches of reality not only enlarges the scope of living, but it sensitises our feel for life and beautifies its quality. Literature scholar Brian Elliott suggests a four-phase approach in shaping such a consciousness.

i. Topographical: What does the place look like?
ii. Ecological: How does life arrange itself there?
iii. Moral: How does such a place influence people? How do the people make their mark on the place?
iv. Subtler: What emotional and spiritual qualities does such a people make their mark upon the place? How does aesthetic evaluation grow?[175]

With such in mind, and with help from learned friends, I offer a more humble 'peer' around the face of the earth… the Australian landscape earth, that is.

★★★

Ancient and Dry Landscape

We live on the third piece of debris from the Sun. A tiny world of rock and metal with a thin veneer of organic matter on the surface,

---

174 Palka. "Grain," 1. Also, Bob Dylan's 1981 song, "Every Grain of Sand" (on the album *Shots of Love*) is well known for its biblical allusions and haunting imagery which has been compared to – and partly inspired by – William Blake's 'Auguries of Innocence'.
175 Detailed in Colloff, *Landscapes of our Hearts* 20-21

The Landscape is...

a tiny fraction of which we happen to constitute.[176] Part of that debris is Australia – an ancient and distinctive land, with animals and plant life that are quite remarkable in their own right.

It is a land unlike any other, weathered to an unimaginable flatness with a consequent vastness of sky, space and light. Ecologist at the Fender School of Environment and Society at the Australian National University (ANU) in Canberra, Matthew Colloff, records:

> Six million years ago, the inland drainage basins of Australia were warm, wet places, dotted with permanent lakes and supporting diverse rainforest. As the climate dried, the lakes evaporated to saline crusts over oxygen-poor black mud. The rivers flowed only during wet periods. Rainforest was replaced with drought-tolerant, fire resistant eucalyptus and acacia.[177]

Although most people consider the Australian continent to be one solid landmass, geologist tell us it is actually more like a giant jigsaw puzzle of at least three former continents that has been put together over many millions of years.

Ancient, yes! The world's oldest rock, a 4.3-billion-year-old zircon crystal, has been uncovered in Western Australia's Jack Hills region, 800 kms north of Perth. According to *Nature Geoscience*, this discovery demonstrates that the Earth's crust formed soon after our planet formed, with the zircon crystal being a remnant of this.

All with a huge, prehuman memory. And with an outback where nature reigns supreme! Space, and freedom. Unspoiled beauty. Except, of course, for open-cut mining and former nuclear weapon sites! But it is also shrouded in mystery and presence especially as experienced by Indigenous/First Peoples of Australia.[178] For Australia's First Peoples, landscape was a ritual, mythic, ceremonial landscape.

---

176 Sagan. *Varieties of Scientific Experience* 5.
177 Colloff. *Landscapes of our Hearts* 60.
178 The earliest scientific evidence of Aboriginal/First Peoples occupation in Australia dates back over 60,000 years.

[F]or tens of millennia before the name Australia was applied to the country there was a clan-by-clan, ceremonial-group by ceremonial-group map of the country.[179]

The Walpiri people of Central Australia have a special word for 'earth'. They call it *jukurrpa*, Dreaming. It is said the Dreaming

> binds people, flora, fauna and natural phenomena into one enormous inter-functioning world... At particular ceremonial sites [they] re-enacted the journey and acts of creation of a particular hero ancestor, and by doing that they sustained the earth.[180]

It is good to be reminded that with around 370 languages and many hundreds more dialects originally spoken in Australia,

> it is impossible to do justice to the wealth and variety of traditional systems of tracking time and seasons. But a recurrent theme is the interconnectedness of human activities and the cycle of changes in flora and fauna that attend the tilting of the earth's axis.[181]

Also worth noting is that, when the First Fleet arrived, the continent was in the midst of one of the most significant El Nino events in recorded history.[182]

But Australia is also more than this. More than a collection of deserts rimmed by a narrow coastal strip. It may have a dry heart – at times achingly dry – that commands respect and insists you pay attention to what is going on around you. Watch, listen, learn. This is not a place to make a mistake.[183] It also has a green 'soul'.

---

179 Keneally. *Australians* 4.
180 Keneally. *Australians* 4.
181 Gaby & Yunkaporta. "The Seasonal 'Calendars' of Indigenous Australia". Monash University, 3 January 2019.
182 Quoted in Karskens, *Colony*, 241.
183 Colloff, *Landscapes of our Hearts* 197.

Green Landscape

During the 18th and 19th centuries, the British colonists and then settlers to Australia lacked the ecological knowledge or connection with landscape beyond the material resources it could provide. Aboriginal people "laughed at the clumsiness and ignorance of the settlers as they attempted to adjust to the new environment". In summer, they would have encountered the full intensity of the Australian sun

> blinding to the eye, burning exposed skin in minutes and forming a heat haze across the hayed-off grasslands... [they] would have suffered in their ignorance.[184]

A bare head or highland bonnet was no substitute for a wide-brimmed hat! Their 'learning' about the landscape focused on its physical layout and on finding well-watered, fertile land

> that could be prepared for farming. 'Improvement' was a remaking of landscape into something familiar and agreeable to them: transforming an impoverished and savage land into a bountiful and peaceful place.[185]

In those early years of colonisation and settlement, both artists and botanists were wrestling with the landscape. In letters and sketches many were unable, initially, to appreciate the beauty and diverse range of environments of the Australian bush. Contradictory responses abounded:

> 'very romantic, beautifully formed by nature...'.
> 'the worst country in the world...'.

The early colonists saw either beauty or usefulness.[186]

---

[184] Colloff, *Landscapes of our Hearts* 82.
[185] Colloff, *Landscapes of our Hearts* 39.
[186] Karskens. *Colony* 243.

By the late 1850s, there was what can only be called a significant change. Of primary fascination in Victoria, for instance, was the Dandenongs, especially the gullies of tree ferns – survivors of Gondwanan – and the huge mountain ash – early settlers called it 'blackbutt' – of Sherbroke Forest. Likewise, Mount Wellington in Tasmania, the Blue Mountains in NSW, and the wildflowers in WA, became centres of botanical exploration and research. And wide-eyed appreciation. Initially interest in tree ferns was on their height rather than their beauty. (Many topping forty feet in some cases.) On a visit to Hobart in 1839, Charles Darwin (1809–1882) remarked:

> In some of the dampest ravines, tree-ferns flourished in an extraordinary manner... The foliage of these trees, forming so many most elegant parasols, created a gloomy shade, like that of the first hour of night.[187]

Others described their encounters with tree-ferns as entering an 'enchanted valley... exquisitely beautiful'... The pursuit of scientific knowledge and aesthetic appreciation went hand-and-hand.

The wonder of giant eucalypts, elegant tree ferns, and the smaller, dainty fern varieties, involved science and sentiment coming together and contributing to an Australian imaginative framework.[188]

Such search for wonder, a cultivated interest in nature, and the ability to describe and present a scene's noteworthiness, provided a way of observing the 'green' landscape of Australia in all its variety.

★★★

---

187 Quoted in Horne. *Pursuit of Wonder* 259.
188 Horne. *Pursuit of Wonder* 279.

Ecological Beauty and Wonder

We are members of the great universe community. We are not on the outside looking in: we are within the universe, awakening to the universe. We participate in its life. We are listening to Earth tell its story...[189] Yes, Earth – a pale blue dot – is our home within the universe. One of the most striking and awe-inspiring nature photographic images of all time is a picture of our very own Earth – known as the Pale Blue Dot – taken on 14 February 1990 by the Voyager 1 space probe, from a record distance of roughly six billion kilometres.

Besides being an incredibly beautiful image, "the Pale Blue Dot gives us some perspective on the scale of our world."[190] What's more, we all share that same Pale Blue Dot. And we carry in our bodies the products of an alchemy, forged in stars billions of years ago.

Earth is a special planet. But that same Earth is changing all the time. It is dynamic. It is our home and one that we should treat with reverence, care, and respect. Especially in the face of the climate crisis. The more we understand our Earth and its part in the 14-billion-year-old cosmos, the more reason we have to stand in awe and reverence at the process which lured and shaped its evolution, our evolution, wherein our existence is rooted... Thus, the beauty of nature is a fundamental aspect of the human relationship with the wider natural world.

When we walk along a sandy beach or trek into a desert, survey the beauty of mountains, a tree fern gully, a summer sunset, or experience a Birdsville luminous night sky – minus city light pollution, the awe and wonder we experience is nature awakening us to the heights and depths of reality which we have neglected.[191]

---

189 Berry. *Selected Writings*, 147.
190 Lau. "Reflections", 3.
191 Barrett. "Pragmatism", 20.

Religion is born out of a sense of wonder and awe. We will recover our sense of wonder and our sense of sacred only if we appreciate the universe beyond ourselves. The landscape. The sky above, the earth below. The grasses, the flowers, the forests, the fauna... To develop an approach called 'loving perception'. To approach so-called lifeless rocks, not to conquer, but to touch... to see the world synthesised in a flower, a sea, or in a human being. Catching glimpses of the whole of reality. Contemplate your own life blended with the total movement of life.

Four years ago, standing on the back deck in his Canberra suburban home, looking south towards Ginninderra Creek, Matthew Colloff reflected:

> To understand our country, non-Indigenous Australians will have to find ways to stop fearing or being indifferent about its physicality and about Indigenous Australians... By attempting to separate ourselves from nature, we isolate ourselves from culture and identity. Instead, a respect and abiding curiosity for the awe-inspiring qualities of landscape and a capacity to predict the moods and behaviours of this land will bring us closer to an understanding of how to live as part of it and, in doing so, become generous of spirit.

So next time you go for a bush walk, pay attention. You will see life in action! And when you see life in action, ask yourself: what is there under the surface that makes life not a solo affair but a dance between partners? And what is there that links this specific instance of life to other lives and to our whole Earth?

It is time to bring 'landscape' back to the heart of deliberations about our future.

8

Looking to Nature: Landscape, Plants and Beauty

"So much depends on how we look at things. The quality of our looking determines what we come to see. Too often we squander the invitations extended to us because our looking has become repetitive and blind. The mystery and beauty is all around us but we never manage to see it. When the imagination awakens, the inner world illuminates. We begin to glimpse things that no-one speaks about, that the outer world seems to ignore"

John O'Donohue

Right now (2023) in my home state of Victoria, but particularly in the *Gariwerd* (also known as the Grampians) on *Djab Wurrung* Country, the hills are alive with wild flowers: Pink Heath, Thryptomene, Blue Tinsel Lily, Flying Duck Orchid, Parrot Pea, Native Fuchsia. Once described as the 'garden of Victoria', the region is home to more than one third of Victoria's flora.

Wild flowers are a beautiful salute to nature. And I haven't got around to mentioning *Kambarang* in WA and *Floriade* in Canberra! But I draw a personal line at the neighbour's smothering Jasmine!

★★★

Some months earlier, we were in Canberra and decided to visit the National Gallery. I particularly wanted to view and experience the Indigenous Art Triennial display called 'Ceremony'. Featured were the works of 38 Aboriginal and Torres Strait Islander artists from across Australia, which revealed how ceremony sits at the nexus of Country, culture, and community. But just before we entered the first of several 'Ceremony' display areas, we passed some other paintings also on display. And among that display were several by the late Australian artist, Margaret Preston (1875–1963).

Having only come across her work in recent years, I stopped to look through the display hoping to see her six-panel work *Australian Wildflowers*. But alas, it hangs in another gallery!

During the late 1920s Preston set out to make Australians see beauty in native flowers, "and gradually they came to dominate her still lifes, sometimes mixed with non-natives, combining English and Australian identities, two hemispheres, and two social eras – one the colonial era of Australia's history, the other the modern era of sovereign nationhood."

She was also one of the first non-Indigenous Australian artists to use Aboriginal motifs in her work. Years later, Preston claimed Aboriginal artists focus "not only on the flower but the whole plant; the roots are of equal importance as the blossoms".[192]

In indigenous art, flowers are about much more than beauty. They engage Country, cosmology, environments, ecologies, totalities of being.[193] Everywhere we look, from the dirt under our feet, to butterfly wings, to the edges of the expanding 'James Webb' cosmos and on every scale from atoms to galaxies, "the universe appears to be saturated with beauty."[194]

◦ Useful or Beneficial beauty – beauty that improves the chances of survival of an organism.

◦ Intrinsic or Useless beauty – beauty that serves no evident purpose "other than to make the natural world inexhaustibly interesting."[195]

---

192 Quoted in Elias. "Useless Beauty" 2.
193 Elias. "Useless Beauty" 2.
194 Sanders. "Useless Beauty" 5.
195 Sanders. "Useless Beauty" 3.

And before you dismiss all this as just extravagant middle-class nonsense, remember that flowering plants are the dominant plants on earth... accounting for more than 81% of all of the planet's biomass. Plants rule the Earth! They are the reason the surface of the planet is not lifeless... Engines of biodiversity! Plants are inextricably tied up with the history of a people. They mirror changes in culture and land use... imported varieties[196] over native, plow, sheep and cattle over bush, housing development, parking lots over wilderness.

With the planet changing so rapidly from human overexploitation, I reckon it is important to remember the wisdom contained in Australian Indigenous knowledge of earth and flowers...

Much more than beauty. An engagement linking Country, cosmology, art, environments, beliefs, ecologies – totalities of being.

★★★

We live on the third piece of debris from the Sun. A tiny world of rock and metal with a thin veneer of organic matter on the surface, a tiny fraction of which we happen to constitute.[197] Immigrants all, the landscape, the trees, the plant life out-age us by millions of years. Our time is but a magpie's warble, long.

Irish philosopher and poet John O'Donohue (1956–2008) reminds us landscape is the first born of creation. No two places in a landscape are the same, and the landscape viewed or experienced from each place is different.[198]

An ancient and distinctive land, Australia has stunning and diverse natural beauty. A land unlike any other... weathered to an unimaginable flatness with a consequent vastness of sky, space and light. During a visit to the MacDonald Ranges in Central

---

[196] According to the *State of the Environment Report* (2021), Australia has more foreign plant species than natives
[197] Sagan. *Varieties of Scientific Experience* 5.
[198] O'Donohue. *Four Elements*, 129, 135.

Australia, Australian ethnographer and author Debrah Bird Rose (1946–2018) wrote of the surrounding landscape:

> Each gorge is a microcosm of life in the desert. One such place of water, life, and red beauty is Trephine Gorge Nature Park. From the parking lot [we] walked through an area thick with the scraggly acacias that Australians call scrub before coming out into a more open area and starting up a path that would take us to the top of the cliff on the western side of the gorge. We scrambled up a steep slope with loose stones, and it wasn't until the track opened out to ledges that formed the top of the cliff that we could stop and look. Suddenly we were face-to-face with the big, exquisite red. Gazing across to the cliff face we were struck again: that dark red stone, those purple shadows, those bands of black, orange, umber. These rocks were ancient....[199]

The oldest rocks in Western Australia, for example, are 4.3 billion years old, almost twice that of the rocks in South Australia, and seven times older than the oldest rocks of the east coast.[200] Yet those deserts soils produce the planet's greatest diversity of flowering plants, with up to twelve thousand species.

The ecological system in which we surely 'live and move and have our being' is the ground that nourishes and sustains us.[201] What we do now, or don't do now, is going to have enormous consequences for the future. Especially around climate change which, as the *State of the Environment Report* (Australia, 2022) clearly indicated, we need to urgently live *differently*.

The beauty of nature is a fundamental aspect of the human relationship with the wider natural world. To see the world synthesised in a flower, a sea urchin, a blue wren or in a human

---

199 Rose. "On the Spot", 220-221.
200 ABC Science. "WA Wildflowers" August 2002.
201 A Japanese study published in *Ecological Applications* suggests that nature around one's home may help mitigate some of the negative mental health effects of the COVID-19 pandemic.

being, is to contemplate your own life blended with the total interconnectedness of life, rather than just staring blankly as if one is an outsider.

> We integrate our mind, our emotions, our body, through the senses; everything we've learned from our culture, the context of the present day, all of that wraps up into our mind. And when we're having a profound experience of beauty, our brain lights up and we are highly motivated to action.[202]

Envisaging the wider reaches of reality not only enlarges the scope of living, but it sensitises our feel for life and beautifies its quality.[203] The cosmos is alive with creativity! The natural world is a vibrant web of radical relationships. Nothing is itself without everything else. "This much is certain", writes Massachusetts professor Chet Raymo,

> the turnip is my cousin. The humming bird and the hump back whale are twigs on my family tree. Bacteria and viruses are my kith and kin.[204]

Radical relationship – the essence of existence. Radical relationship – which require our urgent responses... Protective responsibility. Attentive care. Deliberate nurturing. Such responses echo Indigenous peoples' wisdom. Such responses invite feelings of awe and wonder. Such responses, supported by the 98% of climate scientists, agree that human activity is driving a climate crisis all across the Earth. As environmental philosopher David Orr so eloquently puts it:

> All of us breathe from the same atmosphere, drink the same waters, and are fed from the land. All of us depend, more than we can know, on the stability of the same bioecochemical cycles, including the movement of carbon from plants to the

---
202 Haskell. "Listening", 6.
203 Meland. *Modern Man's Worship*, 288.
204 Raymo. "Distant Cousin" (1985).

atmosphere, oceans, soils, and living creatures... All of us are stitched to a common fabric of life, kin to all other life forms. All of us are products of the same evolutionary forces and carry the marks of our long journey in time... We are all made of stuff that was once part of stars, and we will all become dust to be remade someday into other life forms.[205]

When we quietly sit under a tree "nestling in the curve of the roots in a soft hollow"[206] of grass and gum leaves, or watch a dragonfly dance on water lily pads, the awe and wonder we experience is nature awakening us to the heights and depths of reality which we have neglected.[207] So how should we live in a world overflowing with natural beauty? Keep seeing and keep asking. You will uncover wondrous things![208] It may even dawn on us that we, too, are 'ancestors' and our actions today will have consequences "possibly as broad and far-reaching as the sum total of all the influences that have led to us."[209] Then we can add our own mite of beauty with whatever talent we possess.

★★★

Ceremony is important. Indigenous and First Peoples around the world know that and teach us that. It focuses our attention so that seeing becomes intention. It transcends the boundaries of the individual. It shows respect and reverence. It inspires.

With the Russian invasion of Ukraine still fresh in our minds and TV news, and aware that Ukraine's national flower is a sunflower, what if we shaped a new 'land' ceremony? What if we scattered sunflower seeds all over our neighbourhoods and

---

[205] Orr. *Down to the Wire* ix.
[206] Kimmerer. *Braiding Sweetgrass*, 48.
[207] Barrett. "Pragmatism", 20. While the James Webb Space Telescope now offers 'deep field' images of massive galaxies as far back as 13.7 billion years - just after the Big Bang.
[208] Palka. "Butterflies", 1.
[209] Primack & Abrams. *View from the Centre of the Universe* 294.

communities? And especially in places where tragedies have left a dark void? Would this ceremony not offer comfort, consolation, and beauty to a brokenhearted world? Would this ceremony not offer some gratitude to the Land, to Country, to Culture?

And now a cheeky challenge to Second Peoples... The well-known eco-philosopher, Thomas Berry, is famous for saying one of the best things that could happen today

> is for people all over the world to put their sacred texts in the closet for, say, 300 years and learn again to feel the vital presence of the living Earth and live in healthy, reciprocal relationship with the more-than-human world.[210]

---

210 A quote from Jay McDaniel in *Open Horizons*, "Recovering Pagan Roots".

9

Cultivating a Culture of Reverence

"Without reverence we will gradually descend into ecocide"
Sam Keen

Since discovering his book *Anam Cara*,[211] I have had a bit of a soft spot for the writings of the late Irish poet and priest, John O'Donohue (1956–2008)... as several of the essays in this collection will testify. So I want to commence this essay with some wisdom words from him, lifted from a radio interview he gave just weeks before his sudden death in January 2008. I invite you to read what he told Krista Tippett of *On Being*:

> I think it makes a huge difference... when you wake in the morning and come out of your house, whether you believe you are walking into [a] dead geographical location, which is used to get to a destination, or whether you are emerging out into a landscape that is just as much, if not more, alive as you, but in a totally different form, and if you go towards it with an open heart and a real, watchful reverence, that you will be absolutely amazed at what it will reveal to you.[212]

For O'Donohue, connecting to the landscape in such an elementary yet ordinary moment, was a way of coming into rhythm with the universe.

> Landscape is not just there. It took millennia to come here. Landscape is the first born of creation...[213]

---

211 "soul friend". Appears that Pelagius (ca. 360-430) - a monk from Wales - was the first teacher in the Celtic world to explicitly refer to this spiritual practice.
212 O'Donohue. Radio script, 2007.
213 O'Donohue. *Four Elements*, 129.

Thus my simple thesis: that connection is shaped most creatively when we adopt a lifestyle that follows the advice of the gifters: poets and mystics... Pay attention! Rejoice in it! Care for it! Cultivate a culture of reverence and gratitude!

Kenneth Patton (1911–1994), a poet, artist and respected 'liberal/humanist' from the 1950s, suggested a naturalistic mysticism. Of the mystic experience he stated:

> [It] demands time, the freedom to be absorbed, to forgo practical concerns for the exploring of quality and depth. This is what life should be lived for, these moments of mystical apprehension, for moments of faith and sensitivity.[214]

The capacity of the natural world to inspire a response, albeit a religious response, from humans, has long been recognised. From the mysticism of the ancients to contemporary expressions of wonderment at both the beauty and 'the red claw' of the natural world, it is clear that we humans have always sought to understand our relationship to the universe.

Earth is our platform and its history is our local owner's manual. We are partial products of its approximately four-billion-year-old conditions.[215] Our very existence as Earthlings – being at-home in the universe – is rooted in the fundamental processes of the universe itself...

- out of the stars have we come, says the poet;
- the human story and the universe story are the same story, says the geologian;
- we are not encapsulated, separated, isolated beings, says the cosmologist.

So how can we not stand in awe before the fact of our emergence as a consequence of those same vast processes that created galaxies

---

214 Patton. *Man's Hidden Search*, 118.
215 Fleischman. *Wonder*, 340.

and suns and stars and planets? To stand in awe realising that life takes place under wide horizons,

> horizons that range beyond the span of an individual life or even the life of a nation, a generation... to sense the ultimate in the common and the simple; to feel in the rush of the passing the stillness of the eternal.[216]

The world we inhabit is a circus of forms, of gum leaves and platypuses and human fingers with or without arthritis! Whatever else scientific thinking has contributed, it has certainly amplified the activity and scope of the natural world, away from the *super*natural to the natural. "Taking nature to heart," writes philosopher of religion Jerry Stone,

> does not leave a person with any fewer spiritual benefits than taking to heart the teachings of *super*naturalist traditions.[217]

As mentioned previously, a religious orientation that blends the world-views of both religion and science is called Religious Naturalism – or mystical naturalism as expressed by Bernard Meland. It embraces trackless places and experiences which are different from most traditional Western expressions of religion, such as:

- explores more than one religious tradition;
- seeks to discover the counterpoint between divergent themes within a religious tradition rather than glossing over them;
- acknowledges that such exploration needs to go beyond the official interpretations stated by any tradition, and to push, and – where necessary – reconstruct boundaries;
- encourages an openness or dialogue in which both the self and the tradition is challenged to learn and to grow.

---

216 Heschel. *God in Search of Man*.
217 Stone. *Sacred Nature* 116.

Philosopher of religion Loyal Rue suggests religious naturalists will be known,

> by their reverence and awe before Nature, their love for Nature and natural forms, their sympathy for all living things, their guilt for enlarging ecological footprints, their pride in reducing them, their sense of gratitude directed toward the matrix of life, their contempt for those who abstract themselves from natural values, and their solidarity with those who link their self-esteem to sustainable living.[218]

Thus, wonder and awe when contemplating the immense scale of matter, space, and time, is surely appropriate once we realise we belong to something so very far beyond us. Such naturalistic wonder and awe also counts as deeply spiritual. It is a religious story that whispers of a larger meaning to our existence.

> [W]e are not separate from nature and we are a result of nature's inherent processes... our endless search for insight and understanding cannot be limited in their significance or consequence to the human enterprise alone, but must be part of the emergence of the universe itself.[219]

The crucial task for us is to overcome the objectification of nature.

Science is necessary for good nature writing. Intellectual knowledge can be path to change, But a second major way that writers interpret their/our particular experience of nature is aesthetic attention – sometimes even called 'mysticism' – through image and metaphor. Both arise from our functions of imagination, wonder, and curiosity. Both are essential to comprehending reality.

---

218 Rue. *Religion is Not About God*, 367.
219 Bumbaugh. "Reverence...", (2003).

[M]ysticism is not an abandonment of reason, but a new integration of emotion and reason... and not in any evangelical urge.[220]

All religious traditions,[221] but especially neo-orthodoxy or traditional Christianity – of the Karl Barth and Karl Rahner kind – with its 'otherworldly temper', 'neat doctrines and beliefs' and 'strangeness toward the natural world'...[222] all religious traditions need to re-appreciate that the primary sacred community is the universe itself.

Every other community becomes sacred by participation in this primary community. It invites a larger sense of life. It requires the language of reverence. In moments of wonder we delight in what is. The story of the universe is the new sacred story. What is now needed is new digital-era storytellers, artists, poets and dancers, for unless the story is told and sung and danced, the universe suffers from decay and fatigue. Whether or not we believe that there is something more, nature is so significant that all our beliefs must be reformulated so as to take nature into account.

***

So where to start personally? You can travel outback, or experience the breathtaking panorama of the magnificent Capertree Valley in NSW (that ranks among the largest canyons in the world), or walk along a windswept beach. Go overseas to the Niagara Falls or experience the *Aurora Borealis* at midnight. Many do. And the

---

220 Meland. "The Mystic Returns", 157.
221 "Muslims are far more impressed by the regular rhythms of nature than by the supernatural miracles celebrated in the Jewish and Christian scriptures, because in the Qur'an the natural order is the revelation of divine power and wisdom". (Armstrong, *Sacred Nature*, 120).
222 My local Baptist Church's roadside pulpit declared at the beginning of the week: "Troubled world? Have faith in an afterlife with Jesus". Some days later they changed it: "...have faith in a hereafter with Jesus". (4/2024)

experiences of awe and wonder are profound. But we can also start in our own back yard, or the vacant block next door, where small but complex ecosystems of plant and animal life take hold. Or, stroll through an avenue of maple trees in March and April and witness Autumn's rainbow alleluias. Or, gently rub our hands on a moss-covered rock. Moss... persisted for 450 million years. Or, catch the morning sunrise over a nearby hill on your return home from night-shift.

Nature inviting us to appreciate daily experiences of wonder. To become real members of the earth community. Because, as has been suggested by both philosophers and poets, the way in which we relate to the world as something sacred is by renewing our sense of wonder. "Wonder is not just a fleeting experience of something novel," writes environmental studies professor Lisa Sideris,

> it becomes part of who you are, it becomes part of how you look at the world and, in that sense, not only is it good for you but it can be good for the natural world and for pro-social and pro-environmental kinds of tendencies as well.[223]

★★★

Philosopher Donald Crosby has a story of an ordinary brown pelican,[224] wings outstretched in flight. Scarcely a flicker of those magnificent wings is required for it to soar further and further aloft. Then... it gently banks and slowly descends, only to be uplifted again in its circling flight. For me, a similar sight is a regular occurrence living on the NSW Central Coast as I do now.

Crosby continues his reflection,

---

223 Quoted by Susan Barreto in "Awe, Wonder, and the Religious Roots of America's Ecological Awakening" *Covalence Magazine*. 20 October 2023. Lutheran Alliance for Faith, Science and Technology.
224 The Australian pelican (*Pelecanus conspicillatus*) is predominantly a white bird with black wings and a pink bill. It has the longest bill of any living bird

this pelican's flight is a compelling symbol of the numinous powers, presences, and wonders of the natural order to which we both miraculously belong.[225]

He goes on to tease out how this natural event was religiously meaningful to him. It was a reminder that the self, the pelican, and all other living beings, share in a universe that has enabled us to come into being and to live in accordance with the distinctive traits and capabilities nature has conferred on our respective species. It brought into vivid awareness the evolutionary processes that formed the universe over billions of years. It spoke of the exuberance and joy of life. An image of hope, aspiration and freedom.

But the pelican's flight also symbolised a more precarious side of life. Especially of nonhuman life forms that can be adversely affected by the choices, actions and enterprises of human beings and human institutions. "None of these statements or others", shares Crosby, "can do justice to the firsthand experience itself and all that it meant to me at that time and continues to mean."[226]

We need a new earth-reverent belief system which whispers not that the holy became human in one place at one time to convey a special message to a single chosen people,

> but that the universe itself is continually incarnating itself in microbes and maples, in humming birds and human beings, constantly inviting us to tease out the revelation contained in stars and atoms and every living thing.[227]

Reverence is the capacity to perceive the sacred, to sense that there are entities larger and more important than the self to which one accords awe and gratitude. In past times philosophers of religion scholars called it 'being at-home' in the universe. Because soaking in the brilliant flourishing around oneself, both

---

225 Crosby. *More than Discourse*, 3.
226 Crosby. *More than Discourse*, 6.
227 Bumbaugh. "Reverence...", 2003.

intellectually and emotionally, is a precondition not merely for survival but for the articulation and development of our deeper selves, as earthlings.

Theistic persons traditionally offer reverence to a *super*natural deity. Theistic naturalists conceive of g-o-d as the creative process within the universe. Non-theistic persons are called to revere the whole enterprise of planetary existence. As the words of the epigraph which headed this essay suggest, without reverence we will gradually descend into ecocide.[228]

In short, we must make nature central to any belief system, with any number of earth-focused ceremonial days and liturgies[229] all serving as regular reminders of what we owe our home planet. Following the rhythm of nature through the seasons offers a way of understanding what it means to be human and recognising our inherent place in the ecosystem and the world.

We don't need to look for *super*natural revelation. Sacredness is not opposed to naturalness. Even Irenaeus (ca. 140–202) taught that! We simply need to recognise the sacrality of everything around us. Poet Mary Oliver (1935-2019) agrees... Sometimes I need / only to stand / wherever I am / to be blessed.[230]

Deprived of nature with its beauty, multiplicity, mystery, complexity and otherness, our imaginations would shrivel up, and we would lose our ability to perceive and experience the deeper feelings and intuitions that give real meaning to our lives.[231] All life on Earth, including human life, is tied to the environment in which it lives, and that environment is not static. Thus, the most

---

[228] London. "Renewing our Sense of Wonder..." Interview. Also Brussatt, Interview.
[229] See my Communion liturgy: Banquet of the Cosmos.
[230] Oliver. *Evidence: Poems*.
[231] An observation made by former Australian priest, Paul Collins, in "Religion is poetry or it is nothing!". (ABC Religion & Ethics 2010) when remembering Thomas Berry.

imperative undertaking in life, call it one's religion or philosophy of life, "is the endeavour to adapt oneself courageously to the facts of existence and thus prepare to live the life of integrity."[232]

So next time you go for a nature walk, pay attention. It's called 'appreciative awareness'. You will see life in action! And when you see life in action, ask yourself:

- what is there under the surface that makes life not a solo affair but a dance between partners?
- what is there that links this specific instance of life to other lives and to our whole Earth?

If you keep asking, you will uncover wondrous things![233] Unpredictable. Uncharted. Mindful connectedness. "Not only do we share more than ninety percent of our genes with other primates," writes David Bumbaugh,

> our genome structure is not markedly different from fruit flies or mustard plants. Our beings are intimately related to every living thing that creeps, or crawls or flies, to every living thing that is rooted in the earth and reaches for the sun, to every living thing that inhabits the dark depths of the oceans.[234]

Life becomes loveless and diminished when shorn of its stars at night, and dandelions in our nature strips... of soaring birds, forests, rivers, flowering gardens... we become impoverished in all that makes us human.

---

232 Meland. *Modern Man's Worship*, 254.
233 Palka. "Butterflies", 1.
234 Bumbaugh. "Reverence...", (2003).

10

Old Trees, Wonder, and Orwell's Roses

> *"The planting of a tree, especially one of the long-living hardwood trees, is a gift which you can make to posterity at almost no cost and with almost no trouble, and if the tree takes root it will far outlive the visible effect of any of your other actions, good or evil."*
> George Orwell

You don't have to go into Darlinghurst (Sydney NSW) to the Australian Museum – even though it is the fifth oldest natural history museum in the world – to see an impressive work of art. Go outside and look at the trees! Especially seek out any of the bark shedding Angophora – a native tree and a close relative of the Sydney Red Gum. Known for its clusters of white flowers in December, January and February, and its two different kinds of leaves,

> it's the bark that is so extraordinary. It's flaky and peels off, revealing a wonderful salmon rich red colour and some trees are even redder and richer. Its common name is rusty gum... and that's because it is so rusty looking. Just an extraordinary tree.[235]

Nature's magnificent living sculptures... in our house gardens, on nature strips, in National Parks and bush reserves. Fabulous flora but so often easily overlooked.

★★★

---

[235] 'Angophora', *Gardening Australia*. ABC TV. 11 March 2006.

Trees are some of Earth's most wondrous time capsules. Reach out your hand and touch a tree's trunk. The concentric rings within their trunks – 'wild clocks' – record years and seasons past, many hundreds of years in the making. And invite our obligation to protect its future. Stand under a big old tree and look up. The tallest trees in Australia are all eucalypts, of which there are more than 700 species. Australia's oldest tree is a clonal male (*Lagarostrobos franklinii*) Huon Pine, in Tasmania that is 10,500+ years old, with individual stems 1,000 to 2,000 years old).[236]

Big old tress have always fascinated me. Right from the time as a young boy I learnt to climb some of their more juvenile and smaller offspring on our annual camping adventures to the Grampians (*Gariwerd*) in country Victoria. While a once-only trip to the Victorian Dandenongs – and Sherbroke Forest – was a special treat because towering mountain ashes,[237] potentially reaching up to 330 feet when fully grown, could be seen. But visitors are always warned: Think twice before you enter a forest of ash. 'Widow makers' they were called – sky-scraping, shallow-rooted, loose-limbed gum trees.

> Above all... you have to remember that these trees are time bombs. In dry times their deep leaf litter turns to tinder, and those long ribbons of bark dangling from the branches where they have snagged function like fuses, ferrying sparks up to their open and oil-laden crowns... [When the mountain ash forest does burn] the conflagration is more explosive than that of any other forest fire. Perversely, it is only by means of a really

---

[236] "If you accept a clonal life form as a tree, even that ancient Huon age pales into insignificance against the 43,000-year-old King's Holly (*Lomatia tasmanica*), also found in Tasmania. Once you accept that a common, genetically identical stock can define a tree, then the absolute "winner" for oldest tree (or the oldest clonal material belonging to a tree) must go to the Wollemi Pine (*Wollemia nobilis*). It may be more than 60 million years old." (*Brack & Brookhouse* 2017).

[237] The early settlers called them 'blackbutt'.

violent crown fire, preferably once every three hundred years or so, that a new generation of mountain ash can germinate.[238]

Now, big old trees are disappearing – fast. As recently as three years ago, *Sustainable Timber Tasmania* started to register and map the top 200 giant trees in that State. And they found the second tallest tree in the southern hemisphere was just 20 metres from the edge of a road, and they didn't even know it was there. No sign. No track in. It was just there! Part of the purpose behind the tree register was to assist the tourist industry, so long as such tourist activity was managed. 'We want to get everyone out looking at these trees and partaking in nature...'

One psychology researcher says he is concerned that the growing interest in more contact with nature generally, and with trees specifically, relies too much on only experiencing them visually. Visual contact is important: the claim is that it is an impoverished view of what it means to interact with the natural world. We need to deepen the forms of interaction with nature and make it more immersive. While another has claimed:

> We have entered the urban century, with two-thirds of humanity projected to be living in cities by 2050... There is an awakening underway today to many of the values of nature and the risks and costs of its loss... This new work can help inform investments in livability and sustainability of the world's cities.[239]

Size really matters with trees. Tasmania is second only to California (USA) as being the global hotspot of giant hardwood trees. And a giant tree is a tree more than 85 metres (278 feet) tall or 280 cubic metres in volume. It is claimed the annual net ecological benefit of planting a large species tree is 92% greater than planting a small one.

---

238 Campbell. *Face of Earth*, 276.
239 Robbins. "Ecopsychology", (2020).

Until there is acceptance that large trees, taking decades to reach maturity, have significant value – a fact based on scientific evidence – we will continue to see spurious but convenient assertions that higher numbers of small replacement trees are adequate compensation to facilitate development.[240]

Sadly, Australia – including Tasmania – has an unhealthy tree-felling and pulping tradition.

★★★

Despite Socrates' (c.470–399BCE) claim that 'trees and open country won't teach me anything', trees are very important, and such comment would have scant coherence

> within an indigenous hunting community, for the simple reason that such communities necessarily take their most profound teachings or instructions directly from the more-than-human earth... In indigenous, oral cultures, nature itself is articulate; it speaks... There is no element of the landscape that is definitively void of expressive resonance and power: any movement may be a gesture, any sound may be a voice, a meaningful utterance.[241]

As a species, trees have been in existence for around 370 million years. Do you know that...

(i) trees can taste the air – and insect saliva? When under attack from pests, some trees can identify different insects by their saliva. The trees release pheromones that warn other trees, and sometimes summon other insects that prey on the attacker.

(ii) trees help one another through a 'wood-wide web'? When you walk through the bush, there is a network beneath your feet. Parent trees nourish their saplings through roots, and with the

---

240 Gagen. "Keeping", (2021).
241 Abram. *Spell of the Sensuous*, 116, 117.

help of symbiotic fungi, roots connect neighbouring trees to share nutrients and warnings about threats.

(iii) trees are social beings? A tree on its own can't establish a consistent local climate. But together in a clump or forest they create an ecosystem

> that moderates extremes of heat and cold, stores a great deal of water, and generates a great deal of humidity. And in this protected environment... can live to be very old.[242]

(iv) that some species of eucalyptus trees may hold the key to research into potential degenerative brain disease? Such research is underway at the Yarralumna Nursery in the ACT, 'to explore the anti-inflammatory and anti-fibrosis properties pinocembrim, found in a unique species of eucalyptus trees'. "Trees give form to the land," writes Fenner School of Environment and Society (ACT) ecologist, Matthew Colloff,

> They confer colour and smell and define the feel and look of a place. Through the cover of their canopy and the shade it casts – scattered, dapple light or dark and all enveloping – they moderate the temperature of the land, buffering against winds and extreme heat, and cooling us by the evaporation of water from their leaves... Their leaves are factories for the most important chemical reaction on earth: photosynthesis, the transformation of energy from the sun into chemical energy via the conversion of water and carbon dioxide into oxygen and glucose.[243]

Over the course of their lives, trees store up to 22 tons of carbon dioxide in their trunks, branches and root systems.[244] So put simply: every walk in the bush or through a park is not only good for us... research suggests that being around trees is good for our mental and

---

242 Wohlleben. *Hidden Life of Trees*, 4.
243 Colloff. *Landscapes of our Hearts*, 212-222.
244 Wohlleben. *Hidden Life of Trees*, 93.

social well-being. It is like taking a shower in oxygen! But only by day. Trees don't photosynthesise at night, so they're not exhaling oxygen through their leaves then.

One of my surprises when checking some tree stories was to note that in 1936 George Orwell (1903–1950), later of *Animal Farm* and *Nineteen Eighty-Four* fame, lived in a cottage in Hertfordshire and planted a garden of five fruit trees, seven roses and two gooseberry bushes, all for 12 shillings and sixpence![245] That any socialist, pragmatist or practical person might plant fruit trees is not surprising. But to plant a rose... that can mean so many other unexpected things.[246]

★★★

Trees are among the most powerful beings on the planet. Solid and magnificent, they cover and hold together a third of Earth's surface.

> Their cooling, oxygen-laden breath insures the existence of the rest of life. They are full of magic and mystery. They exert their power both spiritually and literally, with vast under- and above-ground connections to the life of the planet.[247]

Trees are an invitation to think about time and to travel in it the way they do, by standing still and reaching out and down.

Trees are part of our universal natural heritage.

Trees, especially giant trees, are also gems of wonder.

---

245 Writing about his sixpenny each purchase of "two ramblers and three polyantha roses", in the *Tribune*, Orwell later said: "This brought me an indignant letter from a reader who said that roses are bourgeois, but I still think that my sixpence was better spent than if it had gone on cigarettes or even on one of the excellent Fabian Research Pamphlets."
246 Solnit. "Every time...", (2021).
247 Crawford. "The Majesty of Trees" (9.2024).

Old Trees, Wonder, and Orwell's Roses

A sense of wonder is a form of courage, because we all have tendencies to dismiss whatever is puzzling, and to believe whatever is socially sanctioned, soothing, and acceptable.

In our encounters with the broader parts of nature – we are thoroughly nature – we watch the world become new things in new ways... When we hear that a friend has had an experience of wonder, we expect it to remain important to them. We expect to see photos. We expect to hear about ongoing reading and study and possible return visits.

> Wonder beckons... [it] refers to experiences that catalyse urgent, ongoing consideration. Life is lived in buzzing huddles. Generic, plain-vanilla cosmic space does not support life.[248]

Wonder fosters life by encouraging fresh insight.

A favourite poet of mine and others is Mary Oliver (1935–2019). Her poem called "When I Am Among the Trees" is a reminder of our connection with these gentle giants among us.

> When I am among the trees,
> especially the willows and the honey locust,
> equally the beech, the oaks and the pines,
> they give off such hints of gladness,
> I would almost say that they save me, and daily. (*First verse only*)

So sometime during this week, go outside and literally sit under a tree. Go outside and realise that we're surrounded by genius! Look up and say, what is this tree doing that we need to do in our industrial/technological/social media world to meet our needs? Here are a few clues:

---

248 Fleischman. *Wonder*, 110, 111, 311.

- There are solar arrays. And they're not flat on top of a roof, they're in vertical arrays. They are tilting as the sun moves across the sky.
- It is defending itself against pests.
- It is pulling water hundreds of feet up.
- The roots are exchanging nutrients with the roots of the tree next door...

We are immersed in life, whether or not we are aware of it. This is just as true through the cold winter as it is in the warmer/hotter parts of the year. The celebrations of the vernal equinox and of Easter remind us of this in a beautiful way. Nature rises, she rises indeed. But Nature was always here. She never went away! It's just that some of her children did, and they are now coming back![249]

I invite you to both explore and enjoy the wonder and presence of trees. Because, as has been suggested by both philosophers and poets, the way in which we relate to the world as something sacred is by renewing our sense of wonder. Who knows, perhaps on your next walk in a park or the bush you will discover for yourself wonders great and small! And then, following some additional advice from George Orwell:

> it might not be a bad idea, every time you commit an antisocial act, to make a note of it in your diary, and then, at the appropriate season, push an acorn into the ground.[250]

---

249 Palka. "Nature is Rising" (2023).
250 George Orwell. "A Good Word for the Vicar of Bray".

11

Awe and Spirituality of Nature

"The most beautiful thing we can experience is the mysterious. It is the fundamental emotion that stands at the cradle of all true art and science. He to whom this emotion is a stranger, who can no longer wonder and stand rapt in awe, is as good as dead, a snuffed-out candle..."

Albert Einstein

In the first six months of 2024, thousands of people around parts of the world have been 'looking up' to the sky. Two special feats of nature have occurred. A total eclipse of the sun followed by a display of Southern lights. Both were awe inspiring.

On 8 April 2024, colleagues in America experience the eclipse of the sun. As J. D. Stillwater wrote in the *Religious Naturalist Association Newsletter*,

> A total eclipse[251] is hard to describe. It's unsettling, surprising, joyous, connective, astronomical, beautiful, breathtaking ... [L]ike many natural phenomena, it is awesome in the original sense of that word. Like many astronomers, psychological researchers that study the experience of awe also use words like "spiritual" and "religious," because the effects of awe on our brains and bodies are so similar to what religious believers describe and experience at the heights of religious passion.[252]

To view the eclipse, he was located in the grounds of the Neil Armstrong Air and Space Museum (in Wapakoneta, Ohio, the birthplace of Apollo 11 astronaut Neil Armstrong) with a few thousand other people. He continues:

---

[251] A total eclipse occurs on average every 18 months when the dark silhouette of the Moon completely obscures the bright light of the Sun.
[252] Stillwater. *RN Newsletter*, May 2024 1.

It was a friendly, diverse crowd, filled with happy anticipation. We had surprisingly clear skies, perfect for an eclipse. When totality squeezed all the daylight out of the world, the crowd made an odd sound, a guttural cry, as though "breathtaking" meant the heavens forcefully drew the breath up through thousands of vocal cords simultaneously. I felt a deep kinship with the sun, moon, earth and the people around me...

Another observer of the event wrote:

What I didn't expect was the rush of emotions I felt when it happened. I remember goosebumps rising as ripples of light raced through the neighborhood as the moon moved in front of the sun... and the afternoon went dark. I remember dogs barking and yelping, their hair on end. I remember birds going quiet, thinking it was night. The oohs and aahs and other exclamations indicated that this was a shared experience of shock and awe. It was tremendous, mysterious, and terrifying all at once.[253]

While a third person reported:

Many of us who were in the path of totality during the April eclipse watched breathlessly for the moment when the moon completely engulfed the sun, turning day into night. The rarity and spectacle of the eclipse forced us to notice with heightened acuity: the drop in temperature, the quieting of birdsong as the crickets and bullfrogs began their night calls; the three-hundred-and-sixty-degree sunrise. We were wonderstruck.

About a month after the 2024 eclipse, Australian stargazers were treated to some amazing light sites. Solar lights. Southern light sites, or as they are officially known *Aurora Australis*. One Sydney media reporter described the event as

---

253 Moring. "Don't Do Awe Alone. Here's Why". *Orbiter Magazine*, (2017).

Stunning pink and green hues were seen dancing in the sky across Tasmania, outback Western Australia, and along coastal regions of Victoria and South Australia once night fell.[254]

The response generally was one of Wow! Indeed a professor in astronomy went so far as to describe the light show – bigger than anything seen in Australia in decades – as 'bloody awesome'.

It was absolutely spectacular... An 'oh, wow' moment. I was looking at reactions of astronomers in the world and there was one – well-known in the field – who was brought to tears by it.

After viewing the site from his home, he drove to a bayside centre for a better, clearer view. Hundreds of other stargazers were there – many grabbing great photos on their smartphones.

★★★

What was being experienced in both the Eclipse and the Lights was the emotion of 'awe'. Awe is central to the experience of religion, politics, nature and art. Fleeting and rare, experiences of awe can change the course of a life in profound and permanent ways. While philosophers and religious scholars have explored awe for centuries, it was largely ignored by psychologists until the early 2000s. Since then it has become an increasingly popular topic of interest for social science researchers.

So, what is awe? My dictionary tells me awe dates back to Middle English, and was borrowed from Old Norse, a Scandinavian language. Generally speaking, awe – an intense and usually positive emotion – is the feeling of being in the presence "of something

---

254 Tamsin Rose. "Aurora australis offers second chance of 'bloody awesome' southern lights display on Sunday" in *The Guardian*, Sunday 12 May 2024 (on line)

vast that transcends your under-standing of the world."[255] Such experiences tend to shift our attention away from ourselves, make us feel we are part of something greater than ourselves, and more generous toward others. When goosebumps may ripple down one's neck. Or, in broadcaster and author Julia Baird's case, it was her morning swim encounter with a cuttlefish swimming in the wild, astounded by how prehistoric and alien it looked. "For me, [the three-hearted doughnut-shaped brain] cuttlefish are symbols of awe", she said.

> After my first sighting, I was charged with a peculiar kind of electricity for hours. They still have this effect on me. I regularly spend the winter admiring them, then mourn when the spring tides cast their light white bones onto the shore.[256]

While there are several 'flavours' of awe,[257] I guess my particular interest is beauty-based awe which may be elicited by a natural 'scene' (e.g. waterfall, a rainforest, a Manta Ray) or artwork (e.g. Albert Namatjira's Ghost Gums or Monet's Water Lilies). Polish-born American Jewish mystic and Rabbi, Abraham Joshua Heschel (1907–1972) explains:

> The meaning of awe is too realise that life takes place under wide horizons, horizons that range beyond the span of an individual life or even the life of a nation, a generation, or an era. Awe enables us to perceive the world intimations of the divine, to sense on small things the beginning of infinite significance, to sense the ultimate in the common and the simple; to feel in the rush of the passing the stillness of the eternal.[258]

---

255 Keltner. "Why Do We Feel Awe?" in Greater Good '*Mind & Body*', 10 May 2016.
256 Baird. *Phosphorescence*, 20.
257 The 'flavours' of awe include five experiences: threat, beauty, ability, virtue, and supernatural causality. (Keltner and Haidt, 2003. "The Art and Science of Awe").
258 Heschel. *God in Search of Man*, 75.

Awe is not an everyday experience. "You don't wake up awestruck," writes Sarah Laskow.[259] But astronomers and psychological researchers claim we do experience awe a lot more frequently than we think. Seeing maple leaves changing from green to yellow and brown, then pirouetting to the ground. Watching a storm rise across a lake, rippling the surface. Hearing a sudden loud clap of thunder. Standing at the foot of a waterfall being 'baptised' in its spray. All nature-based experiences which can nurture strong connections between individuals and their environment.

About ten years ago, a research study was conducted focusing on the remote and unique Kimberley region in north-western Australia. Visiting tourists were interviewed to determine their most awe-inspiring experience and why. The results highlighted five distinct facets: marine fauna (whales, lemon head sharks), aesthetics, ecological phenomena, vast geological landscapes (cliffs, Montgomery Reef, the Horizontal Falls) and reflective/perspective moments (need for careful infrastructure placement, such as ports, oil and gas installations).[260]

In another recent study, while participants listed nature as their most common elicitor of awe, such experiences were not exclusively nature-based. Other experiences included "scientific works, works of art and the achievement of human cooperation."[261] Many also feel a sense of awe in response to religion, art, music, watching the first human to set foot on the moon, or meeting a popular sporting personality.

Awe puts our own selves and stories in perspectives and turns us toward our interconnectedness with things larger than ourselves. Without that broader perspective, communities cannot survive. Taking the time to experience awe – whether through engaging

---

259 Laskow. "The Mind-Bending Science of Awe" in *Atlas Obscure*, 15 August 2017.
260 Pearce. "Nature-based Tourism Research", (2016).
261 De Cruz. "The Necessity of Awe", 3.

with nature, enjoying great art or music, 'or even bingeing on breathtaking *YouTube* videos' – may not only be good for our minds, bodies and social connections, it may also be a pathway to improving one's life and relationships. That research and others like it has now enabled 'Eight Reasons Why Awe Makes Your Life Better' to be extracted. They are:

1. Awe may improve your mood and make you more satisfied with your life
2. Awe may be good for your health
3. Awe may help you think more critically
4. Awe may decrease materialism
5. Awe makes you feel smaller and more humble
6. Awe can make you feel like you have more time
7. Awe can make you more generous and cooperative
8. Awe can make you feel more connected to other people and humanity[262]

Prior to the current batch of research, conservationist Rachel Carson (1907–1964) also identified awe as a source of resilience in difficult times.

> What is the value of preserving and strengthening this sense of awe and wonder, this recognition of something beyond the boundaries of human existence? Is the exploration of the natural world just a pleasant way to pass the golden hours of childhood or is there something deeper? I am sure there is something much deeper, something lasting and significant. Those who dwell, as scientists or laymen, among the beauties and mysteries of the Earth are never alone or weary of life. Whatever the vexations or concerns of their personal lives, their thoughts can find paths that lead to inner contentment and to renewed excitement in living.[263]

---

[262] Keltner. "Awe and Small Self". *American Psychological Association*, (2017).
[263] Carson. *The Sense of Wonder*, 98.

Simply put, awe is unique in that it encourages people to disengage from their normal focus on the self and the social world, and instead take in the world around them. The studies point in one direction: nature is not only nice to have, but it's a have-to-have for physical health and cognitive function.

★★★

In the old religious language, awe was nearly always about sacred, or divine, or the God g-o-d. *Super*natural. Never about nature. In keeping with that language, the 1921 edition of *Dictionary of Religion and Ethics* defines 'awe' as:

> A feeling of reverence involving actual or potential dread induced by some object of event suggesting sublime mystery. Awe is as aspect of religious experience due to the consciousness of contact with the divine.

Such language sought to direct people's attention upwards, away from things earthy and horizontal towards things invisible, eternal and vertical. Everything was very hierarchical. Cathedrals were built narrow and high. We needed to look long and up. Way up! And it was up – on the ceilings – that many famous religious themed paintings could be found. The Sistine Chapel – the large papal chapel built by Pope Sixtus IV within the Vatican between 1477 and 1480, for instance. Likewise, the Shah Mosque located in Iran, dating from 1611 and regarded as one of the masterpieces of Persian architecture in the Islamic era.

And when the fire toppled Notre Dame's iconic spire and most of its ancient roof in 2019, millions of hearts around the world were broken. The Paris cathedral – constructed over a 200-year period – is one of the most awe-inspiring monuments ever built... Another spectacular symbol of gothic architecture and human achievement. The sheer size and stunning verticality of the place made people feel small and humble, even inducing a sort of spiritual trance-like state.

Today, 'awe' and 'sacred' have returned in a newer religious language. And it's not the same kind of 'sacred'. This shake-up has resulted in a shifting of religious attention, from 'heaven above' coupled with *super*natural persons and doctrines, to 'this world', including flowers, autumn leaves, being moved by music, the ominous rumbling of thunder, sunsets, mountains and desert spinifex. Being at-home in the universe. Because soaking in the brilliant flourishing around one self, both intellectually and emotionally, is a precondition not merely for survival but for the articulation and development of our deeper selves, as earthlings.

Experiencing awe also seems to make us more inclined to help someone in need. And feeling less entitled and self-important while orienting our actions toward the interests of others. Awe says: Notice the wonders and beauty all around you; Care for and be connected to others; Become less individualistic, narcissistic. Noticing. Because noticing shines a light on the particulars

> so that we can be in awe of what we miss; what is worth remembering and returning to when the blur of life becomes stagnant and unimpressive. Seeing is a function that orients us in a place. Noticing nourishes the soul.[264]

★★★

Melbourne academic David Tacey argues "God in Australia will not be proud, haughty or exalted but, rather, everyday, horizontal and earthy."[265] Some years later, he expanded his comments:

> The God of the old-style religion is remote, detached, interventionist and supernatural. The God of the new spirituality, however, is intimate, intense and immanent. This is not to say that spirituality's God is not transcendent and

---

[264] Elle Harrigan. Host of Instagram @livingwildwisdom focusing on mindfulness, creativity, and spirituality through encounters with nature.
[265] Tacey. *ReEnchantment* 256.

sublime, but that this transcendence is imagined differently, not through miracles and magic, but through the radical presence of divine being. God is not conceived as an extrinsic or outside super-reality, but as a mystery at the core of ordinary reality... The new God is everywhere and in all things, or to be more precise, all things are in God (*pan-en-theism*).[266]

The divine, or the sacred, or the god G-o-d – however we use those words – is not aloof and detached and supernatural, but rather is at hand, naturally. Numerous other scholars have been articulating alternative ways of doing theology and reading the biblical texts. Among them is Australian biblical theologian Norman Habel, well known for his work over 60 years on eco-theology during which he was the initiative behind both the liturgical 'Season of Creation' and a 'green Bible'. Accompanying the newer religious language around 'awe' and 'sacred' is the language of 'the spirituality of nature' and a green reading of the Bible. Habel amplifies:

> To be green **is to have empathy with Earth because I know myself as a child of Earth.** To be grey **is to view nature as a resource for humans to exploit because I assume humans are superior to the rest of nature.**[267]

Imaginative and mysterious experiences; mountain top and nature experiences... touching nature and feeling its presence and its other life; awe experiences... all allow us to balance our personal selves with the sense we are in a context that is larger and more important than our selves, and which help to orient us in our lives and in the cosmos.[268] A reverence for the spectacular whole of which we are a part. Being connected with the way things are in all their exciting particularity. And the 'particularity' of the sacred is:

---

266 Tacey. *Spirituality Revolution* 163-164.
267 Habel. *Inconvenient Text*, xix (Bold text in original).
268 Goodenough. *Sacred Depths of Nature*, 174.

in the beauty of the universe around us, and our ability to apprehend it,

in the close encounters with new life and death,

in a special way during a period of suffering,

in praying and meditation,

in church and synagogue contextual liturgies.

We don't need to look for rarified supernatural revelation. We simply need to recognise the sacrality of everything around us. Biblical theologian Norman Habel again:

> The mystery of life deep within nature challenges us... The more I reflect on this mystery of life as we know and experience it on Earth, the more I discover spiritual dimensions to it...
>
> May the atmosphere,
> the moist breath of God enveloping us,
> penetrate every pore of our planet
> and activate all those impulses needed
> to keep our forests green,
> our swallows singing,
> and our dragonflies dancing.[269]

Whether or not we believe that there is something more, that is, nature (with or without the God g-o-d) – is so significant that all our beliefs must be reformulated so as to take nature into account. This will require us to abandon our primary understanding of Earth as a natural resource for unlimited human use and to cultivate, a primary understanding of Earth

---

[269] Habel. *Rainbow of Mysteries*, 116-117.

as the source whence we were born, the nourishment that sustains us while we are living, our healing in moments of distress, and the way to our final destiny.[270]

★★★

Kevin had just walked out of a park onto a paved footpath when he was suddenly stopped by a bird's song. He tracked down the sound to a small black bird standing on a bush between the park edge and the concrete path. He stood very quietly near this bird, marvelling with wonder and awe at what he was witnessing. And then something even more wondrous happened, the bird hopped its body around until it was facing him! This bird then

> puffed up and sang their song a few more times, after which this small wonder hopped back around to their original position. It was as if this bird acknowledged my respectful presence and appreciation of their song: they turned toward me, offered a few notes in my direction, and then turned back. I could only bow to this bird in deep gratitude as I continued on my way and left them to their song-weaving.

Of that experience, Kevin went on to write:

Attending to the places we live and the beings with whom we share these places, with caring attention and respect – by slowing down enough to appreciate the lives and forms which surround us every day and may even want to engage with us – can offer us opportunities for simple and meaningful encounters which can broaden our awareness and deepen our connection to the places and beings with whom we live.[271]

---

[270] Berry. *Sacred Universe*, 168.
[271] Kevin. "Kindred Relationality: The Core Essence of Wild Spirituality", *The Center for Wild Spirituality*, June 2024.

12

Reverencing Water, Womb of Life

"To stand at the edge of the sea, to sense the ebb and flow of the tides, to feel the breath of a mist, is to have knowledge of things that are as nearly eternal as any earthly life can be."

Rachel Carson

The 'Australia Day Honours' 2021 were (again) full of controversy. Especially the Companion Order of Australia (AC) awarded to former tennis great, and now fundamentalist Pentecostal pastor, Margaret Court. The protests... not for her prowess as a former sporting champion but for her outspoken language and views – repugnant to many Australians – on homosexuality, conversion therapy, same-sex marriage, and transgender people.

Within hours, several outstanding Australians returned their Australia Day awards, some from previous years. Among them were Journalist Kerry O'Brien; Medical doctor Clara Tuck Meng Soo; Minister of Religion Alistair Macrae; and Artist Peter Kingston. Kingston is best known for his paintings that capture the energy of Sydney Harbour, and for his environmental activism that helped save several harbour-side icons.

> I am returning my award because I believe the elevation of Margaret Court is contrary to the integrity and meaning of the award and her effort in amplifying divisive opinions has not made our community a better place and contradicts the objectives of the award.

He could have added some additional words from former Uniting Church National President, Alistair Macrae:

It is utterly disingenuous, in this day and age, to claim that Mrs Court's sporting achievements can be separated from her highly publicised comments about LGBTI people... Religious faith has private as well as public ethical dimensions. As a minister and theologian, I am aware that bad theology kills people.

While not down-playing such genuine protest, with which I also happen to agree, such extensive media coverage over-shadowed another Australia Day award recipient, Indigenous elder, artist, and educator, Dr Miriam-Rose Ungunmerr-Baumann AM for being named the 2021 'Senior Australian of the Year'. She is perhaps best known for her reflections on *dadirri*, "inner, deep listening and quiet, still awareness"... something like what we call 'contemplation'. In a speech on *dadirri*, which she gave in 2002 when Principal of a Catholic primary school in Daly River in the Northern Territory, she said

> *Ngangikurungkurr* is the name of my tribe. The word can be broken up into three parts: *Ngangi* means word or 'sound', *Kuri* means 'water', and *kurr* means 'deep'. So the name of my people means 'the Deep Water Sounds' or 'Sounds of the Deep'... We are River people.

Her comments continue...

> When I experience *dadirri*, I am made whole again. I can sit on the riverbank or walk through the trees; even if someone close to me has passed away, I can find my peace in this silent awareness.[272]

Deep water sounds... As the son of the fisherman who spent many days and hours on Pine Lake's edge (in country Victoria) chasing after the illusive red-fin silver fish, and as a mystical naturalist/religious naturalist, that is contemplation I can relate to...

---

272 Ungunmerr-Baumann. "Living Water", (2021).

On Australia Day. On any day. But especially on this day – World Water Day.

Held on 22 March every year since 1993, World Water Day focuses on the importance of freshwater. This year's theme (2022) is 'Valuing Water' as it seeks to raise awareness of the 2.2 billion people living without access to safe water. And it is about taking action to tackle the global water crisis.

While recognised as the driest inhabited continent on earth, with ten named deserts and 70% of the land mass classified either arid or semi-arid land, Australia does have many river systems and fresh water lakes. I am told there are at least 439 rivers – the longest being the *Murray River* (2,375km), while the largest freshwater lake is *Great Lake* in Tasmania. It has an area of 158 square km, measures 22 km by 11 km, and fills a shallow depression averaging 12 metres in depth. As others have said... there's nothing quite as tranquil as a lake. There's something about the still water that forces your brain to relax... Dadirri?

> You cannot touch the same waters twice
> because the flow that has passed
> will never pass again.

When much of this essay was the text for a sermon/address at a local congregation on Storm Day as part of the Season of Creation, I was to preside, preach, and conduct a Baptism... Ah, yes. Baptism, where the primary symbol is water. A lot of water or a small amount of water. But water. As my Baptism liturgy says: 'For us in Australia, the driest continent on earth, water is a precious commodity. Water is everything. Water is life.'

Water. Two hydrogen atoms and one oxygen atom.[273] But where did they come from? Karl Peters (1939-2025) explains:

---

[273] Earth is the only object in our solar system that now has liquid water on its surface.

all hydrogen atoms were formed about three hundred thousand years after the 'big bang'. This was my beginning, my birth – and the birth of you and everything else – all from the initial creative act, the incomprehensible inflation of incomprehensibly high energy. The initial inflation lasted only three seconds, and then the energy continued to expand, creating space-time.[274]

But there is something more than just two atoms: their interaction. Take ice for instance. It forms when the molecules 'stickiness' overcomes their movement. Take water: it forms when the molecules are just right they can overcome the 'stickiness' issue. Take steam: it forms when the molecules' velocity are high enough that collision seldom allows 'stickiness'. Layman's chemistry, I acknowledge, but none of these properties is displayed by individual water molecules. What matters is their relationship.[275] A composite structure that is 'something more' than the original separate attributes. On the other hand, Matthew Fox, of creation spirituality and *Original Blessings* fame, has a different take on this birth of new forms.

> The Universe was not created by tolerant dualisms but by mutual interpenetrations. Of course, this implies letting go: hydrogen must let go of it hydrogenness and oxygen of its oxygenness when the two come together and create water. Letting go is demanded as much of religious traditions as it is of individual religious believers.[276]

★★★

I was running early for the Sunday morning gathering where I was to preside and conduct two baptisms so I drove down to one of my local beaches – Ocean Beach on Broken Bay (Central Coast

---

274 Peters. *Christian Naturalism*, 27.
275 See Goodenough & Deacon (2007).
276 Quoted by Susan Coppage Evans in *Order of the Sacred Earth*, 207.

NSW) – and sat in my car near the surf club tower, car windows down, watching and smelling the waves – ocean water – embrace the sand on the shore. While not 'still water', the gentle rhythm of ocean, its colour and its song, was relaxing and peaceful. And the early morning 'saunterers' were enjoying the water and waves embracing their toes on their morning walk. "All the early stages of life took place in water," professor of philosophy and history Peter Godfrey Smith reminds us.

> ... the origin of life; the birth of animals, the evolution of nervous systems and brains, and the appearance of the complex bodies that make brains worth having... When animals did crawl onto dry land, they took the sea with them. All the basic activities of life occur in water-filled cells bounded by membranes, tiny containers whose insides are remnants of the sea.[277]

My Sunday morning water was quite different to the water and weather some months before. Storms had lashed the coastline, dumping trees and branches, seaweed, plastic rubbish, mud, a refrigerator – some reports said up to 100,000 items – much of it coming from the flooded Hawkesbury-Nepean (*Dyarubbin*[278]) River system which flows into Broken Bay. Fierce winds. Angry dirty water... Tons of it. Wave after wave after wave. Forming and collapsing, time after time. The process was endless. Conditions were dangerous. Flooding[279] was the order of the day due to extreme rainfall – up to as much as 24 inches (600mm) in seven days. Some 18,000 people were evacuated with 1,000 rescued from flood waters by the SES around Sydney and southern parts of the Central Coast.

---

277 Smith. Quoted in Baird. *Phosphorescence*, 21.
278 "Dyarubbin has one of the longest-known human historian in Australia. Aboriginal people have lived there for at least 50,000 years, their ancestors arriving well before the last Ice Age". (Karskens 2020: 2)
279 The floods occurred less than 18 months after Australia was affected by the Black Summer bushfires impacting many towns still recovering from the previous disaster.

But on this day all that was behind me and our Central Coast community. The small wave crests were blue, capped in fair-linen white. The harmony of sun, water, sky, breeze, sand, clouds. The whole experience of nature brought me into the present moment. In wonder. Now I was prepared! And as I drove back towards the church, I remembered some more lines from my Baptism liturgy... 'In the touch of this water, the ancient symbol of new life, I baptise you...' Even some words from a poem:

> Tumbling over
> rocks
> and fallen logs,
>
> water makes music,
> creates beauty,
> breathes in air,
> and nourishes
> more life.[280]

★★★

Over forty years ago, world famous oceanographer and marine biologist, Sylvia Earle,[281] visited Melbourne for a conference about ocean exploration. She recalls standing on the shore of Port Phillip Bay with a young reporter who thrust a microphone under her chin and fired a series of questions. 'Suppose the oceans[282] dried up tomorrow. Why should I care? I don't swim. I hate boats. I get seasick! I don't even like to eat fish. Why should I object if some of them – or all of them – go extinct? Who needs the ocean?' Groaning silently, Earle says, I thought, 'Good grief! Can she be serious?'

---

280 From "Flowing with Obstacles" by Kai Siedenburg.
281 Story retold in Morgan & Garrett. *On The Edge*, 25-26
282 It is claimed the oceans cover nearly three-quarters of the Earth surface, which spurred British fictional writer Arthur C. Clarke (1917-2008) to quip: we shouldn't call our planet Earth at all, but Ocean.

'Right, dry up the oceans. Think of all the good stuff lost at sea that you could just scoop up. The trouble is, there wouldn't be anybody around to do that. Without the ocean, there would be no life - no people, anyway...

'Well, how so?' the journalist prodded. 'People don't drink saltwater?

'Okay... Get rid of the ocean, and Earth would be a lot like Mars. Cold, barren, inhospitable. Ask those who are trying to figure out how astronauts can live there. Or, how about the moon? There's a place with no bothersome ocean. And no life. Or Venus. Yes, the beautiful – and lifeless – hot planet with no ocean.

'It doesn't matter where on Earth you live, everyone is utterly dependent on the existence of that lovely, living saltwater soup. There's plenty of water in the universe without life, but nowhere is there life without water... No blue, no green.'

In our daily lives, we need water all the time. We need it to cook and to clean. In the morning, fresh water on the face washes away sleep and wakens us to the new dawn. Indeed, the human body is composed of over 90 percent water. Science informs us that approximately 71% of the earth's surface is covered by water, by ocean – a continuous body of water that is customarily divided into several principal oceans and smaller seas. Oceans[283] dominate life. All of life has come out of the sea. Scientists claim that life within the ocean evolved some three billion years prior to life on land.

---

283 Note: The Southern Ocean is wild and dynamic. It experiences Earth's strongest winds and largest waves. It is home to city-sized icebergs and the biggest ocean current on the globe, as well as tiny turbulent flows that fit inside a teacup. It is also crucial to Earth's natural systems. It forms the dense water that fills the world's deep oceans. It stores heat and carbon resulting from human-caused global warming, and controls the flux of heat to the huge ice sheet of Antarctica--the greatest threat to runaway global sea-level rise.

The matrix of life began in the primal soup that stirred in the beginning. Here life was spawned. Life crawled out of this water onto land.[284]

Those same scientists also estimate that 230,000 marine life-forms of all types are currently known, but the total could be up to 10 times that number. But... the oceans, the sea, that 71% of the earth's surface is changing due to global warming. Just four years ago, a Report called *'The Oceans are Warming'* prepared by an international team of 14 scientists and published in the journal *Advances in Atmospheric Sciences*, was released. In part, the Report said:

> "The world's oceans are now heating at the same rate as if five Hiroshima atomic bombs were dropped into the water every second. [It] showed that 2019 was yet another year of record-setting ocean warming, with water temperatures reaching the highest temperature ever recorded."

The authors also concluded that as the upward trend is relentless, "we can say with confidence that most of the warming is man-made climate change." The changes required could hardly be more fundamental!

★★★

Philosopher and religious naturalist Donald Crosby suggests that the sacredness of nature is primordial. "Nature as a whole," he says,

> and in its every particular aspect is sacred and can be judged to be *miraculous* in the sense of arousing... a persistent sense of awe and amazement.[285]

In his important essay "Master Symbols of the Ultimacy of Nature", Crosby draws one's attention to the appropriateness of

---

284 O'Donohue. *Four Elements*, 50.
285 Crosby. *More than Discourse*, 86.

'water' as a symbol of the awesome character of nature. He offers three images: a cascading *waterfall*, an adjacent *stream/river* that rushes away from it, and finally enters into a quiet *lake*.

> I propose that we view this scene, not just as an enticing aspect of nature, but as a symbol of the whole of it.[286]

• Waterfall: symbol of the formidable powers of nature, powers of surging creation, and enigmatic of the dazzlingly beautiful things of earth

• Stream/River: suggests by its turbulent flow the ever-changing face of our universe

• Lake: symbol of peacefulness, rest, and assurance we may often experience in the presence of nature especially on a misty morning, a sunset evening, or a moonlit night. "It is obvious," Crosby writes,

> that every living being on earth requires regular amounts of water for its survival. Life and water, therefore, go necessarily together... Earthly water does not give a promise of eternal life, but it is essential for mortal life. As such, it is a fitting symbol of nature as the religious ultimate that endures through all change while all of its creatures, including us humans, come into being and pass out of being.[287]

★★★

Water. A substance composed of the chemical elements hydrogen and oxygen and existing in gaseous, liquid and solid states.

Water. The womb of life... in tidal pools, in clay beds, in volcanic vents... life emerging.

Water. It makes up more than two-thirds of our world and our bodies.

---

[286] Crosby. *More than Discourse*, 87.
[287] Crosby. *More than Discourse*, 89-90.

Water. Drinking, washing, cleaning, cooking, growing food. Most precious resource for survival.

Water. Deadly serious for all who live by agriculture in lands with no dependable rivers, or when the rain doesn't come at the right time. Water. Has a cycle that lasts forever...

> The water in our taps and oceans and tears and clouds has been water forever. That means that the water that baptises children has washed over every generation before them. It has bathed the bodies of the dead and the freshly born. It has been cried by saints and thieves. It has quenched the thirst of history's people. And before there were people on earth, this same water carved valleys and coastlines from mountains. It shaped our landscape; it shapes our lives.[288]

On this weekend/day – World Water Day – I invite you to charge your glasses with refreshing water.

And as you raise your individual glass to drink,

> view this simple but necessary act as a kind of ritual recognition and celebration of the religious ultimacy of the natural world in which we human creatures are privileged to live our lives... [and] rejoice in the everyday miracles and wonders of nature, and reverence the whole of nature.[289]

But also... progressive religion's broad contributions to World Water Day are a kind of cosmic recipe for the functioning of all things. As theologian Karl Peters (1939-2025) suggests:

- A recipe for dancing and living in harmony with our world and the various environments that help shape us.
- A call to live humanly and humanely.
- An invitation to hope. Not hope for any time other than this time. But hope for the fullest and the best that human beings together in concert can achieve.

---

[288] Lawrie. "Baptism", (2009).
[289] Crosby. *More than Discourse*, 91.

We become sacred by our participation in the more sublime dimensions of the world about us.

★★★

Religion is born out of a sense of wonder and awe. We will recover our sense of wonder and our sense of sacred only if we appreciate the universe beyond ourselves.

The landscape

The sky above, the earth below

The grasses, the flowers, the forests, the fauna

The water, the earth, the wind and fire...

Religious sensitivity comes from our attentiveness, recognition, and imaginative appreciation of the natural world. Believe it or not, there has been a long and diverse changing tradition associated with baptism in the religious West. Disputations were frequent and common. So how might a Baptism liturgy look and feel if shaped by the 'universe beyond ourselves'?

For several years, a small group of progressives – brave and 'heretical' colleagues, and myself included – have been experimenting with such liturgies. Liturgies shaped by 'horizontal transcendence' instead of 'vertical transcendence'. Natural not *super*natural. One such liturgy which I have crafted from various resources and discussions, follows:[290]

---

[290] A similar liturgy first appeared in R. A. E. Hunt. *When Progressives Gather Together. Liturgy, Lectionary, Landscapes... And Other Explorations.* Northcote, Morning Star Publishing. 2016. The book is now out of print. Author's rights returned.

Reverencing Water, Womb of Life

(NN) in the touch of this water, the ancient symbol of new life,
The presider introduces the first 'natural' symbol: water
I baptise you in the name of
Life who created you,
Wisdom who knew you first,
Hope by whom you shall be sustained,
Delight in whom I pray you to live, and
Love... may you live every day in its embrace
The presider takes the child...
Out of the stars in their flight, out of the dust of eternity,

All **here have we come, stardust and sunlight,
mingling through time and through space.**

Each time we gather in this sacred place
we are reminded that Aboriginal people
have cared for this land since time immemorial,
> loving it as their mother.

Others have also come from many places on earth
and this place has now become home to all.

Respecting the relationship between humankind and
the earth insight of Aboriginal people,
...and introduces a second 'natural' symbol: earth
(N), we place your feet in this soil.

You are a child of the Spirit and a child of the Earth.
You have inherited the responsibility of caring for this earth.
> Cherish it for all creation.

v2   (NN) may the presence of the Spirit of Love in you
be nurtured and constantly affirmed by
> your family,
> your friends, and by
> your church community.

May the sun and the stars
delight and touch your heart with fire
and so may you find passion to be creative.

The celebration/liturgy continues... etc.

At the end of the liturgy, the presider presents *a third 'natural' symbol: fire*

(N), may this candle remind you
throughout your life, of the sage we call Jesus,
who opened peoples' minds and hearts
to see the 'light' of the Sacred within them.

We are thoroughly nature. To claim otherwise is to attempt to place human beings and everything we do in some rare unimaginable realm beyond the universe, thus rendering the power of our origins lost and our obligations vague. "The role of the church in the twenty-first century," claims Thomas Berry (1914-2009)

> is to speak more directly concerning the universe itself as the primordial revelation of the divine. It should be clear that verbal revelation cannot be a primary revelation, since any communication that takes place through language takes on the distortions of the language, the particular social forms of the times, and the complex patterns of historical events occurring during that period. In contrast, the revelation of the natural world directly and immediately awakens a sense of awe and mystery along with a sense of creatureliness. It arouses, as well, a tendency to worship.[291]

---

291 Berry. "Cosmological Trinity", 127.

13

Bread, Wine, and the Cosmos

"The mouth is the place of eating long before it is the place of speaking."
Rubem Alves

"There was a very thin line between courage and foolhardiness," wrote distinguished professor of liturgical studies, James F. White (1932-2004). He is writing about attempts to describe the tradition of sacraments over at least five centuries, and the reforms sought to liturgy over that time. Many have attempted. Few have succeeded. Tradition, stability, ecumenical convergence, preserving the treasurers of the past "and handing on intact to future generations – this is the function of the church where worship is concerned."[292]

For many years, I have been on such a 'thin line' journey so I know and acknowledge the difficulties. Enculturation is one such term for some of those much-needed reforming attempts. The need for such can be clearly seen here in the Southern hemisphere. The liturgical tradition in its Western form

> was mediated to Australia by missionaries and other invaders, developed in the north and is allied to northern climatic and seasonal patterns... The disjunction between time and place – liturgical time and a 'natural' time, northern time and southern place – can at times be profound...[293]

In the twenty-first century, where the interaction between science and religion plus courageous biblical studies and climate change concerns are near world-wide, such lack of liturgical reform

---

292 White. *Christian Worship*..., 55.
293 Burns. "Over the Ocean", 17-18.

runs the danger of any worship/liturgical activity "becoming irrelevant and banal.... and of being locked into a religious or cultural ghetto."[294]

For the sake of such 'convergence', multiple liturgical practices have been suppressed – even labeled by some traditional 'prayer book' Christians as the "idolatry of creativity".[295] Result? We have been left with an over-concern for the orthodox – right doctrine – line of tradition that just cannot stand up to any rigorous New Testament scholarship by 'truth-telling' scholars and clergy. When liturgy is circumscribed by such issues of 'right belief' or orthodoxy, five things usually happen:

i. it enters the bureaucratic system and loses contact with the life and common experience of the people and becomes responsive only to doctrinal concerns;
ii. traditional theological and liturgical language conditioned by the specialist rather than by the storyteller, can colonialise in many hidden ways;
iii. it becomes more and more estranged from the creative minds of contemporary culture;
iv. it presumes orthodox doctrines are true statements, rather than "mediated phenomena, rooted in specific... perspectives that are now passing";[296]
v. it becomes 'unreal' and 'unnatural'.

The general rigidity and authoritarianism of many approaches to Communion need to be addressed as symptomatic of a general problem in church communities. Interestingly enough, when the Church in Wales was authorising new liturgical services

---

294 White. *Christian Worship and Technological Change*, 128-129.
295 Peters. "Liturgy".
296 Horsfield. *From Jesus to the Internet*, 282.

it did not involve the Doctrine Commission or ask it to produce a theological statement from them. It entrusted full responsibility to the Liturgical Commission to produce baptismal and eucharistic services... Renewal happens when people 'break away from the dead hands and dead minds of the past, and are able to see the think creatively'.[297]

Liturgical renewal is not just some 'progressive' thing. It is central to traditional expressions of Christianity, as well as many renewal movements across denominational boundaries. Sadly, too many past efforts have been either confined to the examination and interpretation of specific historic liturgical texts – "a stroll through East Syria in the fourth century, or Geneva in the sixteenth century, or Oxford in the nineteenth century"[298] – or defined in terms of global 'ecumenical convergence'. Revitalisation *per se* does not seem to have been the primary focus.

One such person to issue a challenge to the *status quo* was Westar Institute founder and New Testament scholar Robert Funk, with his 'call to arms' on worship or the Sunday Morning experience. He wrote:

> throw the old forms out and start over [again]... design a new Sunday Morning experience from the ground up... new music, new liturgy, new scriptures, new ceremonies, new rites of passage.[299]

Funk was of the opinion that, due to the old forms having so much baggage attached to them, understanding them differently was all but impossible. So he made a few 'reconstruction' suggestions.

---

297 White. *Christian Worship and Technological Change*, 52, 128.
298 White. *Christian Worship and Technological Change*, 127.
299 Funk. "Editorial", 2.

i. it should square with and thus confirm the modern world as the horizon of our bona fide religious experience;
ii. the experience should include confession: confession of the church's moral failures;
iii. it should have scriptures, selectively chosen, from the Bible and other sacred texts, ancient and modern;
iv. the experience should grant permission to undertake journeys of faith into unchartered territories;
v. be radically inclusive;
vi. should praise new icons who have pioneered the way in new paths of trust and openness;
vii. it should be a celebration of life; and
viii. should support the creation or identification of new music and symbols.

The goal of such a crafting is to arrive at a rich tapestry of language, metaphors, poetry, and design that (i) celebrates life in the present, (ii) can enrich such expressions of naturalistic beliefs,[300] and (iii) reflects we are people *of* the earth rather than people *on* the earth!

The meaning I give to Funk's call is that the liturgical reconstruction needed must go beyond the "intellectual two-step" called "latitudinarianism" – preserving one's intellectual integrity by proclaiming belief beyond literalism, but continuing to use the anthropomorphic language/images of the traditional hymns, liturgy and creeds "in order to remain within the tradition". But as Davidson Loehr continues, "playing this game [still] compromises

---

300 "Underneath the surface of the various layers of Christianity lurk the remnants of religion that focused on nature. For example... we still name the days of the week after the ancient Germanic gods – Sunday for the sun-god, Monday for the moon-god, Wednesday for Woden, and Saturday for Saturn. These relics remain in spite of the efforts of priests to eliminate everything that smacked of superstitious paganism" (*Lloyd Geering*).

our integrity and our religion... [because] it is another example of keeping what we know and what we believe separated."[301]

In the spirit of such a call by Funk, I offer my case.

★★★

Banquet of the Cosmos

Background

My particular interest in this essay is not so much liturgy in general (although I have been doing that for more than 50 years and there is a fair amount on that in the essay) but the liturgical event traditionally called Holy Communion or Eucharist or Lord's Supper, and to promote a move from the mostly supernatural understanding of such events to a 'natural' understanding. Bread and Wine, elements of life on Earth. In solidarity with life. Gifts of the earth. Work of human hands. Natural not *super*natural.

That is, the new liturgical movement to centre on being at home in the universe with *celebration, presence* and *joy*. Such movement stands in sharp contrast to traditional liturgy where the movement is from *confession to pardon* – or the act of paying off one's debt to G-o-d – reflecting a presupposition of *human guilt*. A progressive naturalistic understanding or pathway counters the heavy supernaturalism which has been built into the sacrament. It is a bold rethinking. We are invited to return to our senses, as:

i. There is the physicality of the symbols: bread, wine, water. Such physicality situates human spirituality "in the midst of its carnal, embodied condition." We are thrown into our sensuality.

---

301 Loehr. "Salvation..." (2000).

ii. There is the encounter with ordinary food: bread and wine, which encourages us "to see the simple realities of material presences in a new light."[302] A genuinely ecological approach strives to enter, ever more deeply, into the sensorial present... To return to our senses is to renew our bond with the wider life, to feel the soil beneath the pavement, to sense – even when indoors – the moon's gaze upon the roof.[303]

The focus of the liturgy is simple: There is a need for the religious traditions to appreciate that the primary sacred community is the universe itself, and that every other community becomes sacred by participation in this primary community. We are thoroughly nature. To claim otherwise is to attempt to place human beings – including the Galilean sage/teacher we call Jesus – and everything we do in some rare unimaginable realm beyond the universe, thus rendering the power of our origins lost and our obligations vague.

> The universe is the supreme manifestation of the sacred. This notion is fundamental to establishing a cosmos, an intelligible manner of understanding the universe, or even any part of the universe.[304]

Introduction

This is based on the most recent research and writings of biblical scholars who have investigated and first two hundreds years 'after Jesus before Christianity'.[305] Solidarity rather than belief.

---

302 Braxton. "Sacrament and Sacrifice", 113.
303 Abram. *Spell of Sensuous*, 270-273.
304 Berry. "The Universe Manifests the Sacred", 31.
305 Vearncombe. *After Jesus Before Christianity* (2021).

Thanksgiving

In our twenty-first century thinking and stories of evolution we need to once more come back to an understanding of the universe. We are late arrivals after some 13.8 billion years of universe history, and after some 4.6 billion years of Earth history. On a time scale... we weren't born yesterday; we were born today!

> Our scientific understanding of the universe, when recounted as story, takes on the role formerly fulfilled by the mythic stories of creation. Our naturalists are no longer simply romanticists... in their interpretive vision; they have absorbed scientific data into their writings. A new intimacy with the universe has begun within the context of our scientific tradition.[306]

Bread and White Wine

It remembers the stories around all the meals in the wisdom tradition of the sage Jesus... Born of a woman and the Hebrew gene pool. A realistic picture of the historical/human Jesus... "Whatever conclusion one might end up with about Jesus", writes Canadian theologian David Galston,

> it must be a possible Jesus and not an incredible one. And a possible Jesus is a Jesus situated in his historical circumstances and who did things and said things that a real person could have reasonably believed or done at that time.[307]

In traditional liturgies Jesus becomes the body that is broken or the bloodshed. But he need not. "He is and need only be the teacher who initiated this tradition of table fellowship...".[308] The use of white, rather than red, wine... For many people –

---

306 Berry. "Human Intimacy with Earth", 36.
307 Galston. *Embracing the Human Jesus*, 50.
308 Galston, "Postmodernism, the Historical Jesus, and the Church", 17.

especially progressives – the close association of red coloured wine to blood is no longer acceptable, and reinforces discredited atonement theories.

Banquet

"The central metaphor for the historical Jesus community is the banquet,"[309] claims Galston again, and he offers at least two reasons for this claim:

i. a banquet was more than a party. It was also a forum for exchanging news, holding debate, and sharing food. For the poor, it was a moment of 'good fortune';
ii. a banquet in the life of Jesus was a symbolic act of openness and solidarity with social outcasts.

THE BANQUET OF THE COSMOS
Introduction

Members of the Jesus movements regularly ate a meal together when they met as a community.

It was a characteristic that they had in common with virtually every other social group in their world.

It was considered primary to the early developments in the movements' meal liturgy.

These meal traditions were not about personal salvation or payment for sin.

Instead, they were about actions and offering hospitality, social identity,

and being in solidarity with those around us.

The liturgical movements centred on celebration, presence, and joy.

I invite you into the spirit of those meals...

---

309 Galston. *Embracing the Human Jesus*, 215.

Presentation

Beginnings and endings shape this meal gathering today.
We celebrate a faithful, strong past.
We prepare for a future yet to be conceived.
We call it the rhythm of life.

Thanksgiving

v1   May it be well with you.

All **And also with you.**

v1   Sacred is the cosmos, whirling, expanding, living, dying, yearning for abundance and freedom.

All **We come to this table awe-struck creatures conscious that as we take these few short steps the whole cosmos — gathered up in us — journeys with us, and in us.**

v2   How can we not stand in wonder and awe.
Those same vast processes that created
    galaxies and suns and stars and planets,
    continue to shape our existence...

v1   Out of the Big Bang the stars;

All **Out of the stardust the Earth;
Out of the molecules of the Earth, life .**

v1   Earth was planted with the seeds of its future;
by the sacrifice of our sun,
Earth flowered forth.
In the human species, nature became conscious of itself
and open to fulfilment in thought and word and deed.

All **Blessed be Earth.**

v1   Blessed be Earth.

All **Earth, our home.**

v2	We celebrate the interconnectedness that is our life – all life. 　　Stardust and mountains, 　　the light at dusk and the moment of dawn; 　　and the feathered ones of the air; 　　kangaroo and desert dingo, 　　earth-worm, butterfly, and bacteria; 　　First/Native Peoples and recent arrivals; 　　sacred wisdom of sages, and the consciousness of prophets
v1	Every day we encounter the cosmos.
All	**It is our bodies, our food, our air, our everything.**
v1	One thing is made up of all other things.
All	**Being and beauty flow freely through all the universe in this great procession of life.**

Bread and White Wine

v1	As we gather together to share and eat food we also remember the stories around all the meals in the wisdom tradition of the Galilean sage we call Jesus...
v2	Born of a woman and the Hebrew gene pool, he was a creature of earth, a moment in the biological evolution of this planet.
v1	Like all human beings, he carried within himself 　　the signature of the supernovas 　　and the geology and life history of the Earth...
v2	For just as the Milky Way is the universe in the form of a galaxy, and the Wedge-tailed Eagle is the universe in the form of a bird, he was and we are, the universe in the form of a human.
All	**May we care for our planet. May we nurture this piece of stardust! May we celebrate with the cosmos!** *(Silence)*

Bread is broken several times

v1   And so we remember the living tradition...
How, during a meal, bread would be taken
and after thanks given, it would be broken and shared
    with both friend and stranger.

v2   This piece of bread is the body of the whole cosmos.
Look deeply and you notice the sunshine in the bread,
    the blue sky in the bread,
    the clouds and the great earth in the bread.

The whole cosmos has come together
in order to bring to us this piece of bread.
(Short silence)

White wine is poured out

v1   After conversation, some wine would be taken,
thanks for it would be given,
    and poured out and shared with all those present.

v1   Wine, fruit of the vine, gift of nature.

v2   Since all food is cosmic and born of the sun and photosynthesis,
    sharing a meal of bread and wine
    renders the universe both sacred and intimate.
(Short silence)

v1   Bread and wine,
Elements for life on Earth...
In solidarity with life...

Response

v2   In sharing this banquet, we in our time and place,
enter into a new relationship,

	with sacred wisdom, with the planet, and with one another,
All	**to feel our kinship with all life**, to raise our voice in the service of life,
All	**to love kindness, and to seek justice**, to live in harmony
All	**and awaken to peace.**
v2	May we sense the wonder of what might yet be.
All	**We are part of Earth Earth is part of us.**
v1	And as we consider this Earth, our home,
All	**may we continue to walk upon it gently and with reverence.**

Communion

The Bread and White Wine – with conversation – is served in small groups around the Gathering space.

★★★

So what may be said about Communion from a progressive/evolving/universe perspective? Some suggestions include:

i. Church statements that claim words said and gestures done, around a holy table, were determined by an original (biblical) 'Lord's Supper' by Jesus, are neither helpful nor accurate. Indeed suspect.[310]

ii. The 'historical' Jesus had no idea his open banquets would become the Christian Eucharist.[311]

---

[310] Smith & Taussig, *Many Tables*, 83-84.
[311] Galston, *Embracing the Human Jesus*, 249.

iii. A banquet is not about *believing* something but about *doing* something. And the 'doing' of the banquet is generosity, not debt satisfaction.[312]

For the sake of 'convergence', multiple liturgical practices have been suppressed. We have been left with an over-concern for the orthodox – right doctrine – line of tradition. I feel many of those who operate out of a traditional/orthodox right doctrine perspective do not understand the limitations of their language. Their meanings are encumbered by their words.

It is no longer 'real' for us to keep our eyes focused on anything but the realities of the world in which we live. Needed are bold liturgists who are prepared to explore new metaphors and images and language drawn from the ways we understand ourselves in the here and now, and experience and celebrate our particular part of the world, pervaded as it is by glorious creativity.

---

312 Galston, "Liturgy in the Key of Q", 18.

14

Blowing in the 'Ruah'

"You are comprised of 84 minerals, 23 elements, and 8 gallons of water spread across 38 trillion cells. You have been built up from nothing but the spare parts of the Earth you have consumed...
You are recycled butterflies, plants, rocks, streams, firewood, wolf fur, and shark teeth, broken down to their smallest parts and rebuilt into our plant's most complete living thing.
You are not living on Earth. You are earth."

Linda Starkweather

In a beginning when God created the heavens and the earth, the earth was a formless void and darkness covered the face of the deep, while a wind [*ruah*] from God swept over the face of the waters...[313]

One doesn't need to be overly religious to know that these well-worn words were composed into a *religiopoiesis* – the crafting of a myth or religion – by the early storytellers and scenario spinners of parts of the Judeo-Christian Bible as they sought to express their understanding of the origins of the cosmos. A formless earth, darkness, water... and wind. And, of course, they go on to include light of the sun and moon through to life here on Earth leading to the place of humans. The story of creation.

One doesn't need to be overly 'scientific' to know there is another story... the grand Epic of Evolution told by scientists and cosmologists. A different story, not founded on divine revelation but on carefully researched theory, with measurement to an astonishing degree of precision and repeated experimentation and research. The New Story.

---

313 NRSV. Genesis 1:1-2.

Similar to the biblical story, the scientific story moves from cosmic to intimate – which of course is the reverse of how nature actually works, from simple to complex – and how the myriads of manifestations are all related one to another. Everything in the cosmos shares a common heritage. Everything is interconnected. "We emerged out of the same formative processes that gave rise to other animals, to plants, and to assorted microbes here on Earth" writes retired neuroscientist, John Palka. He continues:

> These same processes also gave rise to the planet itself, to the solar system, to our galaxy, to the rest of the Universe, and quite possibly to other forms of life beyond our Earth. In addition, our lives are intertwined with those other organisms on Earth and totally dependent both on them and on the Sun. The energy of sunlight drives photosynthesis. Everything we eat is dependent on photosynthesis, as is the oxygen we require for life. Our digestion and the decomposition of our wastes are dependent on a variety [of] microbes. The list of independencies that we know about is very long, and new ones are uncovered every year.[314]

Two stories, or foundational myths. One based on supernatural revelation. One based on scientific research. Both telling about the cosmos and the place of humankind within the cosmos. Wonder and Enchantment. Awe and Reverence. Gratitude.... "inviting us to wrap our arms and minds and hearts around this astonishing whole to which we owe our lives and of which we are a part...".[315] But... and to my mind this is a big BUT, one story more than the other, has contributed to our relationship with the land, climate, waters, flora and fauna, being strained.

As Lynn Townsend White Jr. (1907–1987) in his 1966 lecture *The Historical Roots of our Ecological Crisis* pointed out, there is a strong monotheistic tradition of cutting down the sacred groves,

---

314 Palka. "Valuing Nature". *Nature's Depths* 3 June 2018.
315 See Goodenough & Deacon, (2007).

which stripped the natural world of any spiritual meaning. Citing the biblical Genesis creation story, White argued:

- The Bible asserts humanity's dominion over nature and establishes a trend of anthropocentrism,
- Christianity makes a distinction between humanity (formed in G-o-d's image) and the rest of creation, which has no "soul" or "reason" and is thus inferior.

By destroying pagan religions, White claimed, Christianity made it possible to exploit nature in a mood of indifference to the feelings of natural objects. And... that the ecological crisis – global warming, irreversible ozone depletion, massive deforestation, higher than acceptable methane gas concentrations – was fundamentally a spiritual crisis... Christianity bears a huge burden of guilt. A guilt not shared by the other great traditional religions of the world.

An even more direct criticism of Christianity comes from priest and historian of religions, Thomas Berry (1914–2009). In his 2009 published essay "The Christian Future and the Fate of Earth", he doesn't hold back:

> The present disruption of all the basic life systems of Earth has come about within a culture that emerged from a biblical-Christian matrix. It did not arise out of the Buddhist world or the Hindu or Chinese or Japanese worlds or the Islamic world. It emerged from within our Western Christian-derived civilisation.[316]

Warnings by White and Berry and many others since have failed to generate wide-spread action on climate change.

★★★

Growing up with my late teens/early 20s in the 1960s, I remember the impact of the Pop Music charts and one particular song. That

---

316 Berry. "The Christian Future...", 106.

song was "Blowin' in the Wind' written and performed by Bob Dylan. It was released as a single in 1962 and then a year later on the album 'The Freewheelin' Bob Dylan'. He said it took him ten minutes to write the song while in a small café.

It has been described, wrongly I believe, as a 'protest song' – and poses a series of rhetorical questions about peace, war, and freedom. Dylan claimed the song was actually based off an old spiritual 'No More Auction Block', sung by African slaves who fled after Britain abolished slavery. 'I don't write protest songs', he said. But later on, the song was adopted as an anthem for causes from the anti-war movement, to civil rights, to nuclear disarmament.

The song itself deals with various hypothetical questions surrounding the elements of peace, war, and freedom. Its memorable refrain: "The answer my friend, is blowin' in the wind" has also been described as "impenetrably ambiguous: either the answer is so obvious it is right in your face, or the answer is as intangible as the wind". When first publish the lyrics were accompanied by some comment by Dylan.

> There ain't too much I can say about this song except that the answer is blowing in the wind. It ain't in no book or movie or TV show or discussion group. Man, it's in the wind--and it's blowing in the wind. Too many of these hip people are telling me where the answer is but oh, I won't believe that. I still say it's in the wind and just like a restless piece of paper it's got to come down some... But the only trouble is that no one picks up the answer when it comes down so not too many people get to see and know... and then it flies away. I still say that some of the biggest criminals are those that turn their heads away when they see wrong and know it's wrong. I'm only 21 years old and I know that there's been too many wars... You people over 21, you're older and smarter.[317]

---

317 "Blowin' in the Wind' Summary and Analysis". Bob Dylan. LitCharts.

Despite not charting when first released, in 1994 the song was inducted into the Grammy Hall of Fame. Then in 2004, it was ranked number 14 on *Rolling Stone* magazine's list of the '500 Greatest Songs of All Time'. The answer is certainly blowin' in the (*ruah*) wind!

★★★

The Earth is wrapped in 5,600 million million tons of air. And that air contains five major wind zones: polar easterlies, westerlies, horse latitudes, trade winds, and the doldrums. Of those just named, the Roaring Forties – strong westerly winds[318] that occur in the Southern Hemisphere, generally between the latitudes of 40° and 50° south – are probably the most well known in Australia and New Zealand. Actually they are named in the top eight famous winds of the world. And while we are 'down under', the current record for the strongest measured wind gust, not including tornadoes, occurred in Australia in April 1996 during Tropical Cyclone Olivia.

As it bore down on Barrow Island, 'an individual mesovortex within Olivia's eyewall produced five extreme three-second wind gusts', the peak of which was a 407 klm (253 mph) gust.

Poets are often inspired by the wind. Christina Georgina Rossetti is one such poet.

> Who has seen the wind?
> Neither I nor you.
> But when the leaves hang trembling,
> The wind is passing through.

---

318 During the 1600s and 1700s Age of Sail, trading ships from Portugal, Spain and Europe sailed down the west coast of Africa round the Cape of Good Hope on their way to India and the Spice Islands. They found dashing east along the Roaring Forties was a faster way to get to their destination. However, they had to know the right moment when to turn north-east. If they waited too long they could plough into Australia – the continent's western coastline is littered with the wrecks of ships that missed their turning.

And then there is the old fishing wind proverb: "Wind from the West"

> Wind from the West, fish bite the best.
> Wind from the East, fish bite the least.
> Wind from the North, do not go forth.
> Wind from the South blows bait in their mouth.

But what is wind? The element we can't see but all we know of it comes to us secondhand: we only detect it by consequence. Elusive. Shifty. Fugitive – and difficult to ignore. No wonder the ancients dared not ignore the wind.[319] I have been assured by the Royal Meteorological Society that in simple terms, wind is the movement of air. A movement that is caused by pressure differences, which in turn are caused by temperature differences.

> In other words, it all starts with the sun. As the sun warms the earth's surface, the atmosphere warms too. But thanks to our hills and oceans, the heating is uneven, not to mention that the poles receive less solar energy than the equator... The bigger the pressure difference, the faster the air will move.[320]

Toss in the matter of earth's rotation and we end up calling it all our 'global atmosphere'. Put all together, wind is useful to nature, including humankind, in many ways such as the winds from the oceans carry water and bring rain; wind has in important role aiding plants and other immobile organisms in dispersal of seeds, spores, pollen, etc.; energy can be generated from high speed winds – wind became Australia's leading clean energy source in 2019, 'while advancements in onshore, offshore and micro wind turbines mean the country now has more energy security throughout times of drought, and a supply of electricity in remote areas', despite what some conservative politicians want to claim – and wind helps to

---

319 Mahany. *Book of Nature*, 94.
320 Kirsty McCabe. https://www.rmets.org/metmatters/what-wind (2024)

maintain temperature over a landmass. These factors help shape all life on Earth. Positively when the wind is calm – wind speed of <1 to negatively when wind is in cyclone mode – wind speed of 118+ kmh. "Goldilocks style, keeping us not too hot, and not too cold."[321]

In the world of recreation, wind can figure prominently in several popular sports, including hang gliding, hot air ballooning, kite flying, sailing, and windsurfing. But wind can also affect nature and lifestyles in other ways, such as erosion of soil and sand; it can limit tree growth especially on coastal fringes and isolated mountains – strong winds reduce tree growth; and in some parts of the country cattle and sheep are prone to wind chill caused by a combination of wind and cold temperatures.[322]

★★★

Back to the beginnings of that Genesis biblical story. The Hebrew text says 'ruah' which is correctly translated as wind or breeze. But in many published Bibles – New International, King James, English Standard, New Living, Contemporary English – *'ruah'* is translated as spirit. So my use of 'wind' translation in this essay – New Revised Standard plus New American, and the New English Bible which was given to me at my ordination – seeks to honour the Hebrew. Interestingly, some of those same 'different' translations declare that the wind 'fluttered' over the surface... a wonderful poetic image and phrase. Of the power of poetic, Mary Oliver (1935-2019) says:

> Poetry is one of the ancient arts, and it began, as did all the fine arts, within the original wilderness of the earth. Also, it began through the process of seeing, and feeling, and hearing, and smelling, and touching, and then remembering – I mean remembering in words – what these perceptual experiences

---

321 Mahany. *Book of Nature*, 94.
322 Wikipedia. https://en.wikipedia.org/wiki/Wind#: :text=Wind%

were like, while trying to describe the endless invisible fears and desires of our inner lives.[323]

As a natural force, the wind in some religions was often personified as one or more of the wind gods, or as an expression of the *super*natural. Such 'belief' is behind the Genesis opening story in the Judeo-Christian tradition. It is also important to note that in Hebrew the most holy name for God is not a word but a four-lettered symbol: Y, H, W, H which in English is written as Yahweh. "Peeling it back just a bit", writes Barbara Mahany,

> and sounding it out, the first syllable, Y-H, is the inbreath, and the second, W-H, is a whispered outbreath; the whole name a single cycle of breath... a name spoken, as it were, by the wind.[324]

Leading New Testament scholar, Brandon Scott, takes up the 'ruah/wind/spirit debate in a 2023 blog posting called "Blowin' in the Wind". And it's a language thing! The Hebrew word '*ruah*' means wind, breath, air. The Greek word 'pneuma' means wind, breath, air. The Latin word 'spiritus' means wind, breath, air.

> The Hebrew, Greek, and Latin all have the same primary meaning. Wind, breath, and air are all aspects of the same thing and constitute the primary usage in each language. This pneumatic phenomenon has some interesting characteristics. It can be felt but not seen. The presence of breath in a mammal indicates life; its disappearance indicates death. These aspects enable wind-breath-air to function as a metaphor for the presence of the mysterious or divine. This last usage is rare.[325]

But when did 'wind' become 'spirit'? Things changed following the Council of Nicaea in 325CE. "The metaphor became a person,

---
323 Posted on Facebook 'Mary Oliver Poetry Enthusiasts site, 24/6/24, by Steve Merrill.
324 Mahany. *Book of Nature* 95 Also quoting David Abram *Spell of the Sensuous*.
325 Scott. "Blowin' in the Wind" (2023).

the third person of the Trinity", and then developed with a capital H and a capital S! With the result:

> when French and English separated from Latin, instead of translating 'spiritus' as breath, they **transliterated** it, so in French it became esprit and in English spirit. As a transliteration it lost its connection to the physical and metaphorical meaning wind/breath/air.[326]

Transliterations are lazy, wrong and misleading. They lead to a profound misunderstanding. They should be prohibited! So... 'a wind [*ruah*] "fluttered" over the surface... bringing order out of chaos'. As I said previously, a wonder-ful poetic image and phrase. The transmission of ideas and mystery via language. Metaphorical not literalist.

Remembering the words and theses of both Bernard Meland and Thomas Berry, religion is born out of the experiences of wonder and awe. "The great decline of religion in the industrial country," writes Berry,

> can be attributed in large part to the loss of an experience of the grandeur of the natural world, because of our newly acquired technological control over so many aspects of the natural world. At present, we are completely encompassed by the world of human artifice.[327]

★★★

Wind and Rain. Sunshine and the Milky Way. Flora, All beings, and Human beings. And divinity is also of the universe, part of nature, says theological poet Pattian Rogers, "when it is observed and noted and imagined and expressed by creatures, born of nature

---

326 Scott. "Blowin' in the Wind" (2023). Emphasis added.
327 Berry. *Sacred Universe*, 82.

with physical, blood-beating, light-snapping minds".[328] Nature is everything that is. We are not and cannot ever be 'unnatural'. We are not encapsulated, separated, isolated beings. We are always simply of nature.

> I may wander through a community of trees and listen to the breezes blowing through the leaves. I feel the movement of the wind and sense the breath of Life in the air, among the trees and in the lungs. For the trees of the forest are the lungs of Earth. I am aware of the wind, breath, and atmosphere – the spirit we associate with God. It animates us and all life on Earth.[329]

★★★

We must begin to re-imagine our most foundational ways of being. Because there is an urgent need for re-connection and re-membering ourselves back into an intimate relationship with the global web of life.

> Scientists are unanimously agreed that without the blanket of atmosphere that envelops our planet no such creature as man[kind], or any other form of organic life, could exist. And further, when man's finely constructed instruments for interacting with that atmosphere, his respiratory system, cease to operate, that interaction, which we call breathing, stops and death ensues.[330]

---

328 Rogers. "This Nature". Partnership for Earth Spirituality: http://www.earthspirituality.org/archive/ford_seminar.htm
329 Habel. *Rainbow of Mysteries*, 110.
330 Meland. *Modern Man's Worship*, 150

15

Cosmic Life... and Death

"We're alive; we have some modest degree of intelligence; there is a universe around us that clearly permits the evolution of life and intelligence... But what is interesting is that if things were a little different, if the laws of nature were a little different, if the constraints that determine the action of these laws of nature were a little different, then the universe might be so different as to be incompatible with life."

Carl Sagan

Earth, that hunk of space rock and metal with a thin patina – a veneer – of organic matter on the surface, "that orbits a humdrum star in the obscure outskirts of an ordinary galaxy comprised of 400 billion stars in an observable universe of some hundred billion galaxies",[331] a tiny fraction of which we happen to constitute, is four and a half billion years old. It is located in a universe – that whole "complex, interrelated and interacting... matter-energy in space-time... of which humans are an integral part..."[332] of 13.8 billion years.

Due to its distance from the Sun and protection from Jupiter's gravity, that same Earth has a liveable amount of heat and light. The importance of this protection is illustrated

> by the catastrophic effects of the few big impacts that have occurred anyway, the most recent of which about 65 million years ago wiped out the dinosaurs and many other species. If such events were happening much more often, life on Earth

---

331 Sagan. Quoted in Primack & Abrams. *The View from the Centre of the Universe* 274. Also in *Varieties*, 5.
332 Gillette. "Theology Of, By, and For" (2006).

might not have had enough time between extinctions to evolve to intelligent creatures.[333]

And while we are at it, it should also be noted: the orbit of the Earth has been in the habitable zone for its entire life-time; Earth is the only object in our solar system that now has liquid water on its surface; and Earth's relatively thin crust and abundant surface water

> allow continued geological activity – especially plate tectonics moving the continents, forming new mountain ranges and other features, and continually recycling carbon and other elements essential for life.[334]

The universe story... Singularity. Expansion. Inflation. Subatomic particles. Gases. Stars. Lumps of matter. Primordial soup. Life. Catastrophic events. Death. Forever extinction. Living Beings... Why should we not look upon the universe with wonder?

> I hold a rock in my hand and I resonate with its heft and its patterns; I try to imagine its broiling history within the Earth's interior; I rejoice in our co-habitation within the planetary matrix; and I absorb the understanding that our atoms all came from the same stars, and that some of my atoms will come to inhabit rocks and that some of its atoms will come to inhabit lifeforms.[335]

★★★

We are Earthlings... yes, and maybe also *worldlings*. We have a special connection to our planet... 'out of the stars have we come.' We are made of the rarest material in the universe: supernova stardust. In the words of Connie Barlow, one half of the *Thank God for Evolution* team,

---

333 Primack & Abrams. *The View from the Centre of the Universe*, 210.
334 Primack & Abrams. *The View from the Centre of the Universe*, 211-212.
335 Goodenough. *Sacred Depths of Nature*, 39.

Tell me a creation story more wondrous than that of a living cell forged from the residue of exploding stars. Tell me a story of transformation more magical than that of a fish hauling out onto land and becoming amphibian, or a reptile taking to the air and becoming bird, or a mammal slipping back into the sea and becoming whale. Surely this science-based culture of all cultures can find meaning and cause for celebration in its very own cosmic creation story.[336]

Evolution. Emergence. Sacred story. Life and death stories. In poetic/liturgical language of Bruce Sanguin,

> By the sacrifice of a supernova,
> Earth was planted with the seeds of its future;
> By the sacrifice of our sun
> Earth flowered forth...[337]

And as pointed out by others, hordes of past species of life on earth have become extinct in order that new species can arise and flourish over time. "Without such massive extinctions, we humans would never have arrived on earth".[338] The human story and the universe story are the same story. "Our very existence is rooted in the fundamental processes of the universe itself," writes David Bumbaugh.

> How can we not stand in awe before the fact of our emergence as a consequence of those same vast processes that created galaxies and suns and stars and planets?[339]

In similar sentiments, Karl Peters (1939-2025), Professor Emeritus of Philosophy and Religion, and former President of the Centre for Advanced Study of Religion and Science, has said:

---

[336] Dowd. *Thank God for Evolution*, 142
[337] Sanguin. *If Darwin Prayed*, 188.
[338] Crosby. *More than Discourse*, 149. Also Geering. *From the Big Bang to God*..."as a result of five major interruptions to the evolution of life, scientists now estimate that 99% of all living species brought forth by the creative process are already extinct." (p. 49).
[339] Bumbaugh. "Reverence..." (2003).

Our planet, its life forms, and our own bodies contain the oxygen, nitrogen, carbon, iron, and other elements from earlier exploding stars. We are 'star stuff' – a part of the matter that was created earlier in the universe's history.[340]

In an earlier article, also referenced in this chapter, Peters began to explore around this theme a little more than in his *Dancing with the Sacred* by asking a couple more questions about our cosmic 'life', and then suggesting some answers of his own.

'How old are we?' His response:

[p]henomenally, a few decades; culturally, a few centuries or millennia; biologically, millions of years; cosmically, about 15 billion years.[341]

How long will we continue?' Peters response:

[p]henomenally, a few more decades or less; culturally, maybe a few more centuries; biologically, millions of years or, if we do not destroy ourselves first, perhaps until our sun dies five 5 billion years from now; cosmically, until the universe ends, which may be never... It all depends on how we think of our selves.[342]

Peters' answers are a kind of cosmic recipe for the functioning of all things...

★★★

Is Earth alive? Generally speaking scientists adopt the position that all so-called 'celestial objects' including the Earth itself, are regarded as non-living. But it is a position that is being challenged. as others raise the question of whether a planet like Earth, on which life abounds, might appropriately be considered as living. For instance,

---

340 Peters. *Dancing with the Sacred*, 15.
341 Peters. "Interrelating Nature..." 412.
342 Peters. "Interrelating Nature..." 412.

Irish philosopher and former priest, John O'Donohue makes this Celtic-shaped claim:

> ... it makes a huge difference, when you wake in the morning and come out of your house, whether you believe you are walking into [a] dead geographical location, which is used to get to a destination, or whether you are emerging out into a landscape that is just as much, if not more, alive as you, but in a totally different form, and if you have come to understand landscape as something that forms each of us.

Within the world of science, another suggestion has come from James Lovelock and Lynn Margulis, known as the *Gaia Hypothesis*. They proposed that the drama of life

> ... does not unfold on the stage of a dead Earth, but, that, rather the stage itself is animated, part of a larger living entity, Gaia, composed of the biosphere together with the 'nonliving' components that shape, respond to, and cycle through the biota of the Earth.[343]

Debate continues. Neuroscientist John Palka[344] attempts to summarise:

1. The oldest idea is that living organisms inhabit a non-living Earth and adapt to the conditions that Earth provides them.
2. An intermediate idea is that the living and non-livng components of the Earth co-evolve, but you can always tell life from non-life, and legitimately speak of the two separately.
3. The Gaian perspective goes a step further. It emphasises the idea that when components interact as closely as living and non-living components present on Earth do, they constitute a whole. To think of Earth as a single living superorganism, Gaia.

In his words, John Palka then asks: what do you think? He closes with a further quote from David Grinspoon:

---

343 As summarised by David Grinspoon (*Faith in Human Hands*) and quoted in Palka "Is Earth Alive?", page 3.
344 Palka. "Is Earth Alive?" (2017).

When we stop thinking of planets as merely objects or places where living beings may or may not be present, but rather as themselves living or nonliving entities, it can color the way we think. Perhaps life is something that happens not on a planet but to a planet: it is something that a planet becomes.[345]

★★★

Australia has a lot at stake when it comes to climate change. Indeed, humanity has never before faced such a threat: the collapse of the very elements that keep us alive! Australia also has one of the weakest 2030 pledges in the world, compared to other wealthy and high-emitting countries, when it comes to carbon emissions and climate change action. "We've seen the risks dramatically escalate over the past five years," professor Lesley Hughes has pointed out.

> We have much to lose and everything to gain by acting decisively to get emissions plummeting this critical decade. The findings of the most recent IPCC report would be 'dire' and that since the last one, Australia has experienced more 'unnatural disasters'. We must focus on the fact that predictions are now becoming observations.[346]

This is to be expected, unfortunately, as the seeds of this recalcitrant inaction were sewn during the prime ministership of conservative John Howard and the fossil-fuel/greenhouse mafia he took with him to Paris to make ineffective the Kyoto Agreement on climate change.[347] Global warming is *not* a future tense statement. It doesn't just concern our grandchildren. It concerns us. It will not go away despite the babbling mouthings of the right-wing media hacks and politicians. Earth is a precious living habitat. Earth *is* a fragile web of ecosystems. The universe is not a-part from us. We are it. The world is our true home. We are fully

---
345 Grinspoon. Quoted in Palka "Is Earth Alive?"
346 Hughes. "Aim Higher..." (2023).
347 See Hamilton. *Scorcher* (2007).

linked with our surroundings in time, space, matter/energy, and causality, and where the metaphor of 'web' is used to describe this interrelatedness.[348]

> As earth-creatures we do not live in straight lines; we truly do exist in a web, a network, a maze... When the relationality is mutually supportive, and not distorted, we truly can speak of 'mazing grace'.[349]

It is also true that for years scientists have been showing people data in the form of graphs of temperature vs. time, maps of sea level rise, and movies of sea-ice changes. "You'd think this would be enough," laments astrophysicist Adam Frank, "but it hasn't gotten us anywhere near the level of urgency needed to generate quick action." He continues:

> The failure to generate action on climate change has a number of causes, including well-organized science denial. But I believe its root cause is that we haven't yet translated that data into a "big story," a new mythic level narrative about human beings and our place in Earth's 4-billion-year history of life and the planet co-evolving.[350]

One possible solution is to let the poets and storytellers teach new narratives of what scientists can't! Scholarly criticism and abstractions can *inspire* us. But as I have indicated elsewhere, the shaping of any new myth needs both the voice of the critic – to keep any community free from sloppy sentimentality – as well as the concern of the creative artist – to strike a chord and resonate within. Ideally the two should function 'in stereo' – simultaneous

---

348 Some have challenged this understanding because the image of a web is too meagre and simple for the reality. A web is flat and finished 'and has the mortal frailty of the individual spider'. And although elastic it has insufficient depth.
349 Axel. "Reshaping the Task of Theology", 61.
350 Frank. "Climate Change and the Power of Story" (2018).

but different. To substantially change how we feel we may need to participate in *storytelling* as well as some sort of *spiritual practice*. The weaving of story (what we tell) and ritual (what we enact) are ways we make sense of our world. Nature is not a place to visit, it is home! Indeed, our only home.

Another possible solution is to encourage human-level, lived experiences, of the natural world as real. Such action is endorsed and encouraged by religious studies professor Lisa Sideris[351], even when she is a critic of the 'New Story/New Genesis', and many other advocates – such as Loyal Rue, Ursula Goodenough, Connie Barlow, E. O. Wilson, and Thomas Berry to name just a few. Particularly, she claims,

> these narratives tend to encourage awe and wonder at scientific information and expert knowledge as that which is most 'real', over and above direct encounters with the natural world.

However Thomas Berry, for instance, is a strong advocate of such intimacy. He writes:

> Our relationship with Earth involves something more than pragmatic use, academic understanding, or aesthetic appreciation. A truly human intimacy with Earth and with the entire natural world is needed. Our children should be properly introduced to the world in which they live, to the trees and grasses and flowers, to the bird and the insects and the various animals that roam over the land, to the entire range of natural phenomena...[352]

While weekly columnist Chet Raymo is keen to remind us that science cannot and should not be a religion, but it can be the basis for the religious experience. Thus, scientific knowledge adds to the excitement of nature – of the flower. It adds. It does not subtract.

---

351 Sideris. "Science as Sacred Myth?" (2015), 1.
352 Berry. *Selected Writings*, 34.

Around forty years ago, Victoria Loorz launched a different understanding and practice of religious sensitivity which took the 'environment' seriously. She called it *Church of the Wild*. In more recent years, she has authored a book of the same name, and how nature invites us into the sacred. In one of the chapters she has this interesting observation:

> People exploit what they have merely concluded to be of value, but they defend what they love. To defend what we love we need a particularizing language, for we love what we particularly know. This is a courtship of the particular."[353]

Courtship of the particular... A different attitude towards nature lovingly bundled up in four words. The beginnings of a 'new' story of reverence? The deep time, cosmic perspective has allowed us to appreciate the scale and unprecedented nature of recent human impacts on the planet. The universe is also fascinating and awe-inspiring in its own right. Certainly via a 'new' story told by the ones who call us to live in harmony with the whole cosmos/universe/planet, and who remind us that novelty and surprise, coupled with wonder and awe makes life interesting... The unfolding of universal life and our own coming into being – how the Earth made us – as beautifully articulated by British astro biologist and professor of science communication at the University of Westminster, Lewis Dartnell:

> The water in your body once flowed down the Nile, fell as monsoon rain onto India, and swirled around the Pacific. The carbon in the organic molecules of your cells was mined from the atmosphere by the plants that we eat. The salt in your sweat and tears, the calcium of your bones, and iron in your blood all eroded out of the rocks of Earth's crust; and the sulphur of the protein molecules in your hair and muscles was spewed out by volcanoes. The Earth has also provided us with the raw materials we have extracted, refined,

---

[353] Loorz, *Church of the Wild*, 128.

and assembled into our tools and technologies, from the roughly fashioned hand-axes of the Stone Age, to today's computers and smart phones. It was our planet's active geological forces that drove our evolution in East Africa as a uniquely intelligent, communicative, and resourceful kind of ape, while a fluctuating planetary climate enabled us to migrate around the world to become the most widely spread animal species on Earth.[354]

---

354 Dartnell. *Origins*, 1-2.

16

Boney and Spindly! Reviving Liturgy with the Sensuous Textures of Landscape

"At its best, Liturgy is a poetic and eclectic mix of words, action, music and song that is both Aspirational and Inspirational."

Angela P. Smith

I have learnt much about liturgy from my three young grandchildren. And wisdom from poets, among them being Mary Oliver (1935–2019), Dennis McCarty, and the Irish poet and philosopher, John O'Donohue (1956–2008).

Take any three-year-old for a walk, say... along a beach or bush track. Don't plan to be in a hurry.

Every twig or seashell. Every muddy pool of water. Every dragonfly, or small lizard to cross your path will be an occasion for closer 'looking' and 'excitement' and 'wonder'. Children intuitively apprehend the truth that we are all part of nature. Rachel Carson (1907–1964) is well known for her 1960s book *Silent Spring* – the book which documented the environmental harm caused by the indiscriminate use of the pesticide DDT. Around the same time she began writing a small book – *The Sense of Wonder*, celebrating her three year old grandnephew Roger and his discovery of the wonder of nature. Reflecting on those experiences Carson wrote:

> A child's world is fresh and new and beautiful, full of wonder and excitement. It is our misfortune that for most of us that clear-eyed vision, that true instinct for what is beautiful and awe-inspiring, is dimmed and even lost before

we reach adulthood. If I had influence with the good fairy who is supposed to preside over the christening of all children, I should ask that her gift to each child in the world be a sense of wonder so indestructible that it would last throughout life, as an unfailing antidote against the boredom and disenchantments of later years, the sterile preoccupation with things that are artificial, the alienation from the sources of our strength.

If a child is to keep alive his inborn sense of wonder without any such gift from the fairies, he needs the companionship of at least one adult who can share it, rediscovering with him the joy, excitement, and mystery of the world we live in.[355]

So reflecting on Carson's story is important. So too is following the 'advice for living' from Mary Oliver... pay attention; be astonished; tell about it. Because such attention and experience comes from being immersed in what is, and seeing the overlooked. Because such attention is scientifically informed. And because such attention is what helps shape good liturgy.

★★★

Not long having published his first book, *Modern Man's Worship*, theologian Bernard Meland (1899–1993) penned:

When you stand before massive uplifts of rock, mountain-sides, or cascades, or before huge, high trees whose branches reach upward serenely, there is something that lifts you out of yourself. It takes hold of you, too, at the seashore or while at sea, watching the deep waters rise up into great liquid walls. It presses down upon you also when... lying back to the ground, you look your fill into the sky. If you have ever climbed a mountain-side whose paths wind on and on toward lonely heights, each turning separating you farther and farther from the world below, ushering you step by step into a new and strange wilderness where hardly a foot has trod, startling you

---

355 Carson. *Sense of Wonder*, 44, 49.

now and then by the sudden flight of a bird or the crash of a loosened boulder, you know what it means to have "Infinity come down and settle over" you.[356]

Meland suggests, as did Albert Einstein (1879–1955) before him, the natural world has the capacity to inspire a response – an expression of our awe of nature, of our attraction to the mystery of existence, to something intangible – called 'religious' or 'spiritual' from humans. He was highly critical of literalist religion – "the literalist simply will not be reverent before ideas or emotions that transcend his understanding"[357] – and religion that fostered "a sense of strangeness toward the natural world."[358] Referencing his mentor Gerald Birney Smith, Meland stated:

> As long as this emotional barrier persists, the religious man faces a serious dilemma, for until he does become emotionally oriented in the universe, his religion can never be genuinely integrated in the affairs of the natural world.[359]

Likewise, others have said, quite passionately, that there is no good reason to believe taking nature to heart leaves a person with any fewer spiritual benefits than taking to heart the teachings of *super*naturalist traditions.

> If we can go to special places, built by humans, which are designated as sacred, surely we can go to special places, shaped naturally, which are recognized as sacred..."[360]

Religion is born out of a sense of wonder and awe. We will recover our sense of wonder and our sense of sacred only if we appreciate the universe beyond ourselves. The landscape. The sky

---

356 Meland. *Modern Man's Worship*, 270.
357 Meland. *The Reawakening of Christian Faith*, 70.
358 Meland. "Kinsmen of the Wild" 1.
359 Meland. "Kinsmen of the Wild", 443.
360 Stone. *Sacred Nature*, 116.

above, the earth below. The grasses, the flowers, the forests, the fauna... The miracle of each moment awaits our sensual wonder.

Landscape especially has an incredible presence. Landscape is the firstborn of creation/evolution. It was here for hundreds of millions of years before ever a plant or an animal arrived. Thus writes John O'Donohue:

> I often think that our liturgies have become very bony and very spindly and have none of the sensuous textures of landscape in them. Maybe that would be one way of reviving liturgy, bringing it out into the landscape and allowing the elemental force of the landscape to clothe the liturgy again with sensuous texture and enable us to come in.[361]

It is 'landscape' or the 'natural environment' that is the common denominator between all peoples living in that particular location. We are cosmic and we are local. Present-day Australians still have a limited understanding of the mountains, deserts, rainforests; of the ocean and river systems, the fauna and flora, as well as the climate conditions called 'seasons' of the nation. Not to mention any real appreciation of the First Nations 'songlines' Dreaming tradition, probable the oldest continuous sacred tradition in the world.[362] I admit I chuckled at poet Les Murray's (1938–2019) description of the Australian seasons as comprising essentially summer and non-summer. A reign of heat, flies, snakes, beach culture... followed by a cooler time in which the discomforts disappear. And a bit of sniffling cold in the middle.

Australia being an ancient continent located in the southern hemisphere, all of the major traditional Lectionary festivals are out of whack. There is a ritual discomfort! Any celebration is almost done in defiance of their northern-hemisphere reference points. Result? We miss what actually 'is'! Getting more specific,

---

361 O'Donohue. *Walking in Wonder* 55.
362 Tacey. *ReEnchantment* 76.

Australian religious Clare Johnson articulates the problems faced in Australian celebration of liturgy using northern hemisphere sources...

> It is obvious that, because of our global location, southern hemisphere Christians cannot easily relate to and ritualise the feasts and seasons of the liturgical year utilising the same 'natural-world' metaphors, analogies and semiotic interpretations as northern hemisphere Christians. To do so entails a level of mental gymnastics that can prove quite distracting in the context of liturgical celebration or theological reflection... One example of this tendency can be found in... Christmas and Epiphany... The problem for southern hemisphere Christians at hearing the invocation of northern-season-inspired theological imagery... is that in real-world time, we are actually in the midst of summer, when the days are at their longest and the nights their shortest. Light is something we have in abundance in December/January... especially when the glare of the scorching summer sun is at its harshest...[363]

To see the world synthesised in a flower, a sea, or in a human being, is to contemplate your own life blended with the total movement of life, rather than just staring blankly as if one is a tourist or outsider. Such moments not only enlarges the scope of living, but "sensitizes our feel for life and beautifies its quality."[364] The sacred is not a separate '*super*natural' sphere of life. It is more like "the caffeine in coffee"[365] than like a strawberry on top of a pavlova. In the end, the universe can only be explained in terms of celebration. It is all an exuberant expression of existence itself.

★★★

---

363 Johnson. "Relating Liturgical Time to 'Place-time'", 33, 35.
364 Meland. *Modern Man's Worship*, 288.
365 Stone. *Sacred Nature*, 19.

In my book *When Progressives Gather Together* (2016) and on my web site, I offer a collection of liturgies under the heading: "A Gathering Liturgy for the Celebration of Life". That is, I do not call the experience 'worship'. Rather I call it 'celebration'. Influenced by philosopher Sam Keen, I too want to suggest there is a major difference between the event 'worship' and the event 'celebration'.

- *Worship* moves from symbol to a transcendent source – persons, word, places, Holy or G-o-d – present in the ordinary. *Celebration* consists of rejoicing in the presence of things rather than going beyond them.
- *Worship* seeks to transcend the object, such as G-o-d. Hosanna in the highest! *Celebration* seeks insight into the importance of things. Hosanna! Right here. Right now. This.
- *Worship* is only possible where there is a distinction/dualism between the 'sacred' and the 'ordinary'. The relationship is generally submissive – pray, praise, please a deity. *Celebration* seeks to dissolve such distinctions and dualisms...

Religious orientation only lives while we are making it up. While our creative juices are firing and we are 'composting' new angles, new narratives, new metaphors within the particular context of the moment because these things are liberating. Such 'composting' is much more than embarking on a salvage operation. What is required are liturgies that are shaped by a different religious sensitivity.

A sensitivity away from Nicene orthodoxy that has come undone with the advent of the modern world.

Some 'Nature' Liturgies

Perhaps the following liturgies might give some expression to this...

(i) The Church of the Wild

Victoria Loorz has been shaping and co-leading the Church in the Wild for nearly forty years. Her book of the same name shares that story, and towards the end the book offers a series of resources to assist others who may wish to follow in this new tradition. At each gathering the 'liturgy' is shaped accordingly (in outline only)...[366]

• *Gathering and Silence*

Gatherings are conducted outdoors and the silent listening is centred on what's available in that setting. Animals. Fauna. Trees. Insects.

> "Listen to your breath.
> Listen to the wind...
> We aren't just meeting in nature: we are entering into relationship with nature..."

• *Land Acknowledgment*

To acknowledge and honour "the watershed, the land and creatures, and the peoples who traditionally lived on this land for generations".

They are not inviting nature to join them, "we are opening up our own awareness that the trees and jays and clouds are already in a state of worship – simply be being themselves".

• *Sacred Readings* These can include Scripture (from the edges of the Christian tradition), or poems (e.g. Mary Oliver, Rumi), or ancient prayer.

> "But the primary 'readings' come from what Bonaventure called the primary book of revelation, 'The Book of Creation'..."

Those with musical talents are invited to lead or perform songs.

• *The Sermo (or Sermon as Conversation)*

The 'sermo' is divided into three sections.

---

[366] All quotations from Loorz. *Church of the Wild* (2021), Resources section, 200-222.

i. An invitation to wander. "Listen to your body is the place to begin".
  ii. A solo wandering and wondering for a long time (45 minutes), off-trail. "Open up your imagination and intuition".
  iii. Coming back together in the circle to share experiences with the others. "If it feels right, bring a [gift]... a stick, a flower or the rusty tin can..." Gifts are to be placed on the altar and persons invited to share a little about their experience "as we pass this rock around the circle".

- *Communion*

Shared bread and wine symbolising ones commitment to life and the place of sacrifice and death

"A dynamic reminder that we are already one with God".

- *Benediction/Wild Blessings*

A call to "go back to the human world and to bring the lessons of the wild world with you".

Also an opportunity to both affirm and to say farewell.

(ii) The Flower Communion Service

The Flower Communion service had its origins in 1923 when Norbert Capek (1870–1942),[367] a former Baptist and later founder of the Unitarian Church in Czechoslovakia, introduced it to his congregation... A congregation that was made up of former Roman Catholics, former orthodox Protestants and former liberal Jews.

People had experienced a devastating world war and its aftermath, plus many members of the church "found that their religious needs could not be met by the empty ceremonies and the hymns which were part of the churches of their childhood".[368]

---

367 Capek was executed by the Nazis in the Dachau concentration camp in 1942.
368 Bumbaugh in Seaburg (ed). *The Communion Book*, 162.

Capek knew ritual was important, especially in war-torn Europe. But what to do! He turned to nature. Thus, the Flower Communion service was given shape.

Each person was asked to bring a flower of their choice. The flowers were arranged in a vase or basket and taken into the worship space. "Dr Capek then said a prayer, after which he walked over and consecrated the flowers while the congregation stood."[369] A very simple ritual. At the end of the service everyone was invited to take a flower – not the one they brought – thus symbolising their shared celebration in community.

> The significance of the flower communion is that as no two flowers are alike, so no two people are alike, yet each has a contribution to make... By exchanging flowers, we show our willingness to walk together in our search for truth, disregarding all that might divide us".[370]

Since then a potpourri of Flower Communion services have been crafted, shared and celebrated. Most often such liturgies are celebrated in Unitarian Universalist churches around the world, but especially in the USA following its 1940 introduction in Cambridge, Massachusetts, by Capek's wife, Maja V. Capek. What follows in my attempt to shape such a 'spring-time flower' liturgy by drawing on various accounts and liturgies, other sources – Narrative, Progressive Biblical, Religious Humanism, Religious Naturalism, Mystical Naturalism – as well as incorporating a 'progressive' Communion (bread and white wine elements) theology.

---

369 Seaburg (ed). *The Communion Book*, 150.
370 Seaburg (ed). *The Communion Book* 150-151.

The Liturgy (Designed for several Voices)

Introduction *(Optional)*

v1   Members of the Jesus movements regularly ate a meal together
when they met as a community.

> It was a characteristic that they had in common
>   with virtually every other social group in their world.
> It was considered primary to the early developments
>   in the movements' meal liturgy.

> These meal traditions were not about personal salvation or payment for sin.
> Instead, they were about actions and offering hospitality, social identity,
>   and being in solidarity with those around us.

> The liturgical movements centred on celebration, presence, and joy.
> I invite you into the spirit of those meals...

Thanksgiving

v1   The earth has gone the round of seasons:
        from the vibrant green of spring's new life
        to the lush richness of warm summer,
        to the brilliant fulfillment of riotous autumn,
        to the generosity and self-giving of winter...

v1   Now we stand again, touched by the promise
of new life in the spring.

v2   Have you considered the flowers, the lilies of the fields?

v3   They spin not, neither do they sow,

v2   yet Solomon, in all his glory

v3   was not arrayed as one of these.

v2   Say what you will about the economy of life,
     flowers are irrefutable proof
          of nature's extravagance.

v1   Everywhere you look,
     in every nook and cranny,
     during this season of life,
          the flowers are there...

v3   Spilling down a creek bank,
     along a bush path,
     in shopping centre parking lots,
     in outback desert places, where the landscape
          is not just there, it took 4.4 billion years to be there.

v1   Flowers do not bloom for us.
     They do not care whether or not we see them.
          They grow and bloom
          because they are full of life.

v2   They are a gift of grace.
     They invite us to seek the beauty in each moment.
     They encourage us to find fulfilment in life
          and the living of it.

v3   And what nature has done for flowers,
     nature has done for us.
          We, too, are products of nature's extravagance.
          Each of us is unique.

v3   Mingled together,
          interacting,
          we do not lose our uniqueness,
     but rather find our uniqueness heightened.

v1 Here, in this place,
    here in this human community,
        we find the fuller dimensions of our individuality,
        the richer meaning of our existence,
        the profound delight of this world
        and our existence in this world.

v2 As you came into this Gathering this morning,
    you brought with you a flower,
        from your yard,
        from along your street,
        from a florist,
        from your neighbour's flower bed,
        from the cluster near the entrance.

v2 From many different sources
    these many different flowers have come.

v1 Together they symbolise the extravagance of nature,
    for as various as these flowers are,
        they do not begin to exhaust nature's inventiveness
        in creating forms and colours and beauty.

v1 And what nature has done for flowers,
    nature has done for us.

In Solidarity... With Food and Drink and Conversation

v2 In all the colours and scents and tastes and sounds
    of the world, we see the beauty of the universe.

v2 In this season of spring it is fitting we should celebrate
    the renewal of life and hope, using
        the symbols of spreads and biscuits,
        of wine and bread, of coffee, tea, and flowers.

v2 Time out of mind we have watched
    grain buried in the dark soil.

v2   Time out of mind we have watched sprouting seeds
break through the soil, reaching towards the warm sun.

v2   Time out of mind we have watched grain broken,
ground into dust-like flour.
>   Yet mixed with water and leavening,
>   > it stirs, rises, becomes bread, and scones and biscuits,
>   > > sustainers of our lives.

v2   For longer than we can remember
the fruit of the vine has been our companion.
>   Its clustered fruit is harvested
>   > and crushed, and juice is stored and fermented
>   > > saved for festive occasions.

v2   We have shared the fruit of the vine
in moments of joy and sorrow,
>   and to mark momentous turnings.

Sharing (Communion)

v1   And so… We give thanks
v3   And seek to live in harmony with all about us.
v1   We give thanks
v3   And take our place in the human story,
struggling for the unity of humankind.
v1   We give thanks
v3   And join with all in a quest for justice.
v1   We give thanks
v2   And celebrate that we, too, come from the earth,
the same life that has made flowers and creatures,
>   that we might add to the earth's richness.

Food and Drinks and Conversation

If in a progressive Christian setting…
In Solidarity… Communion

Remembering the tradition surrounding Jesus...
we break this bread and fill this cup.
Bread broken. White Wine poured out

We give thanks
- All **And seek to live in harmony with all about us.**

We give thanks
- All **And take our place in the human story, struggling for the unity of humankind.**

We give thanks
- All **And join with all in a quest for justice.**

We give thanks
- All **For all that Jesus, human like us, means to us.**

Bread and White Wine served in clusters (or local tradition)

After Communion

v2   And now we prepare to leave this place.
As you do, you are invited to take one of the flowers.
Take a different one than the flower you brought.
    Take it not to keep forever and forever.
    Nothing is forever.

v1   Take a flower as a symbol of gratitude
    for beauty we did not create,
    for joys which come when unexpected.

v1   Take a flower as a symbol of your participation
    in the community of this gathering,
    in the community of human kind,
    in the community of all living things,
    in the universal community.

v3   In this world we cannot earn or deserve
that which is most important.
    It comes to us as a gift.

v1   If you did not bring a flower take one anyway.
Take a flower as a symbol
>of beauty
>and grace
>and joy
>and love.
For knowing how to receive
is fully as important as knowing how to give.

(iii) Stations of the Universe

And due to the pioneering work of Meland and others, a small group of interested liturgists has been examining the possibility of shaping a 'Stations of the Universe' project – following the Easter tradition in some churches called 'Stations of the Cross'. An initial exciting suggestion/outline is shaped thus... forging a link between naturalism and such feelings of wonder and awe:

1 – The Big Bang
2 – The emergence of the Elements
3 – The formation of Stars
4 – The formation of Galaxies
5 – The formation of the Milky Way
6 – The formation of the Sun and Solar System, including Earth
7 – The formation of Earth's atmosphere
8 – The formation of Earth's oceans
9 – The emergence of life
10 – The start of photosynthesis
11 – The emergence of Animals
12 – The emergence of mammals
13 – The emergence of humans
14 – YOUR birth

Other ritual like-minded engagements, suitable for liturgy and/or meditation groups and eco-spiritual retreats include: a 'Cosmic Walk' (Miriam MacGillis, USA), the 'Cosmic Mass' (Matthew Fox,

USA) and the 'Sacred Energy: Mass of the Universe' (William L. Wallace, NZ).[371]

***

Liturgy that is bureaucratically conditioned cannot serve the spiritual needs of diverse congregations and individuals. Such liturgy:

    i. Loses contact with the life and common experience of the people and becomes responsive only to doctrinal concerns;
    ii. Becomes more and more estranged from the creative minds of contemporary culture;
    iii. Presumes orthodox doctrines are true statements, rather than "mediated phenomena, rooted in specific... perspectives that are now passing."[372]

Liturgy which is a celebration of life, all of life, is shaped by a spirituality that is more horizontal than vertical.

Because... Earth – a pale blue dot as dubbed by Carl Sagan – is our home in the universe. The language and images used will reflect we are people of the earth rather than people on the earth!

Because... nature is the thread that completes the tapestry of life. Natural not supernatural. An experience animated by a sense of awe, wonder, belonging, and relatedness. A Newer Testament. The gospel of the natural present moment.

Because... this is an experimental universe. It is not a place where evolution happens, it is evolution happening![373] Change is not merely an appearance but is essential to the way things are. Life

---

371 Details in my book, *Seasons and Self*, 24.
372 Horsfield. *From Jesus to the Internet*, 282-
373 Peters. "Human Salvation...", (2012)

is animate... continually incarnating itself in microbes and maples, in humming birds and human beings.[374]

Because... such religious and liturgical shaping will likely revere the wisdom of reason, collective human experience, and 'landscape', more highly than any single sacred book or credal tradition. Let there be no doubt: rituals are the core of every strong community's life. But faithfulness to a tradition is not achieved by continually reproducing the same formulations over and over again without significant change.

Sadly, liturgical reconstruction seldom comes from the dominant expression at any one time. When creative ideas for a new future do emerge beyond the contours of Christian orthodoxy, within a humanistic and naturalistic paradigm, for example, they tend to come from the minority explorations of free religious thinking, "not unlike the way yeast works in bread making or a small mustard seed that's sowed in a field."[375]

To escape the charge of 'boney and spindly' liturgy, the job of progressives is to create imaginative liturgical and other religious resources and let future generations find in them what is helpful. Resources. Not mandates. Such offerings, I would contend, can throw life into a new frame. They rend the veil of the ordinary. They demand courage (heart) and new patterns of engagement. They interrupt, and can sometimes transform one's life.

---

374 Bumbaugh. "Reverence..." (2003).
375 Horsfield. *From Jesus to the Internet*, 290.

Epilogue
Living Religiously as a Mystical Naturalist

> *"The More, which earlier mystics viewed as something different from the common sense reality, turns out to be this experienceable world seen in the fullness of its meaning. Modern mysticism, then, has one dogma: see things in their relations, in their amplitude."*
>
> Bernard Meland

Mystical naturalism. A 'wild' faith. Sacred nature. Nature is so significant that all our beliefs must be reformulated so as to take nature into account. This will require us to abandon our primary understanding of Earth as a natural resource for unlimited human use, and change to a primary understanding of Earth

> as the source whence we were born, the nourishment that sustains us while we are living, our healing in moments of distress, and the way to our final destiny".[376]

Victoria Loorz of *Church of the Wild* is passionate about nature. Like Thomas Berry she too writes:

> People exploit what they have merely concluded to be of value, but they defend what they love. To defend what we love we need a particularizing language, for we love what we particularly know. This is a courtship of the particular.[377]

Language is important. Thus the language of 'courtship of the particular' requires us to: Pay attention! Rejoice in it! Care for it! Cultivate a culture of reverence and gratitude! Nature is not a place to visit, it is home!

---

376 Berry, *Sacred Universe*, 168.
377 Loorz, *Church of the Wild*, 128.

> At home not as plunderers and exploiters of nature's resources, but as creatures of earth, born of its processes, nurtured and sustained by the subtle and intricate interchange as humanly evolved organisms within this enveloping atmosphere...[378]

In a recently published essay,[379] I wrote of the celebration of a natural 'wild' spirituality... released from the captivity of *super*natural religion – as an expression of our awe of nature, of our attraction to the mystery of existence, and to something intangible. An important requirement in our times. Important because... celebrating a naturalistic '*wild*' faith is to move away from tradition towards heresy (another opinion) often with radically new approaches and in provocative ways. And important because... celebrating a naturalistic wild '*faith*' is a body energised by wonder and awe and beauty. Paying attention to our experiences and thoughts and emotions and letting them be, is life affirming, even if they're hard. A 'surplusage of experience'. A breathing and acting and encountering that throws life into a new frame as it makes its creative way in the real 'landscape' world. Lyricist Peter Mayer is suggestive:

> We can still create a religion that helps align our hearts and minds, and our actions, with the astonishing beauty that has brought us here.[380]

So two challenging questions remain in my mind: (i) what type of religion and spiritual practices do we need going towards the year 2050 and beyond? (ii) how might a 'wild' faith shaped by mystical naturalism help us to live religiously as a mystical naturalist and connect to nature in our ordinary daily life? I offer some suggestions that might be worth mulling over:

---

378 Meland, "Grace: A Dimension Within Nature?", 135.
379 Hunt. "In Celebration of a 'Wild' Faith: Jesus in the Australian Landscape" (2023).
380 Mayer, *Pro-Future*, 1.

Religion and Spiritual Practices

Any religion emerging in the Anthropocene[381] – be it pantheistic, Pagan, shamanism, Druidry, deep ecology, Christian naturalism, religious naturalism – which is attempted to help make sense of our lives, should at least be:

- grounded in the best cosmological understandings of our world as articulated by 'liberal' modern science, beginning with the epic of evolution;
- an affirmation that celebrates life – the whole of life – in all its diversity;
- non-require of a belief in G-o-d although it may include belief in G-o-d naturalistically conceived;
- prophetic, clearly naming and addressing our world's gravest social problems;
- radically change-oriented as the time remaining is indeed short, if not too late already;
- an eco-religion that regards planet Earth as a sacred living system, and that cherishes and celebrates life with life-affirming rituals...

That is, a religion that considers nature to be sacred, imbued with mystery and intrinsic value, and worthy of reverent care.[382] The downside of such a religion is that one does not have divine intervention, the solace and comfort of a super mind, nor immortality.

> When an earthquake devastates Lisbon, when tsunamis or hurricane strike, or when the depth of human evil is revealed in holocaust, child abuse, torture, or the holds of slave ships, there is no God to cling to. We cannot take refuge in God's will to make sense of it all or rely on God to save us. It is

---

[381] Thomas Berry uses the term 'Ecozoic'.
[382] Bron Taylor calls this 'dark green' religion.

our responsibility to strengthen the levees and prepare for emergencies. It is our job to comfort the bereaved. It is our job to resist genocide and to remember those who perished.[383]

Connecting to Nature in Daily Life

Be encouraged to share in these simple communal practices[384] might be a place to begin... as we move towards regarding nature as sacred.

1. Start where you are

Notice the sunrise, sky, and weather. Breathe in the air. The natural world is part of your everyday life, even in the midst of a city.

2. Go screen free

Take breaks from mobile phones, computers, and other electronic devices, especially when you're outside. Enjoy observing and exploring the world around you.

3. Go for the green and blue

Look for opportunities to be near trees, plants, and water... even a water fountain in a community park. Venture out into green spaces for longer breaks.

4. Make it part of your day

When walking in a park, pause and greet a tree that you walk part most other days. Consider this an essential wellness practice.

---

383 Stone. *Religious Naturalism Today*, 228.
384 As suggested by Kai Siedenburg, a deep nature connection guide, Ecotherapist and poet, in her collection *Space Between the Stones* (2020)..

5. Bring the outside in

Having nature images or natural plants in your indoor environment will help you stay connected with nature and the special places you love.

6. Give thanks

Every day we receive many gifts from the natural world... a sunset, a flower, a dragonfly on a leaf, a refreshing shower of rain, tumbling clouds. Look for opportunities to appreciate these gifts more, even just for a few moments.

7. Share in a Cosmic Walk

Seek out and participate in a Cosmic Walk... and reflect on the scientific fact that we too are part of the universe's billions-of-years-old history.

★★★

By sharing in such 'connections', maybe then we can experience nature as sacred and confront the dark times of dangerous climate change. And any such 'faith' will have to be conceived, at least in part, in terms of wide ecological and evolutionary metaphors. What matters most for the religious life is imagination and experimentation. Engaging the mind *imagining*, not just *thinking*. As a 20th century mystic has said (before inclusive language which I feel he would have embraced):

> Whatever faith men will have after our skeptical age has done, that faith need not be unable to encompass the mystery and complexity of life. If it fails of this, it cannot be the path [we] are seeking. As long as we make our point of departure not

our beliefs but life itself, we are not shut to growth. Life is not words.[385]

So in the tradition of a 'blessing', I pass on these closing encouragements. Each time you fill a glass with water and raise it to your lips to drink, be encouraged to view this simple but necessary act

> as a kind of ritual recognition and celebration of the religious ultimacy of the natural world in which we human creatures are privileged to live our lives, give of ourselves in deeds of service to our human and nonhuman others, rejoice in the everyday miracles and wonders of nature, and reverence the whole of nature. Water reflects... in its every aspect and role the religious ultimacy of nature.[386]

And... changing a line from the vehement anti-Nazi German playwright and poet, Bertolt Brecht (1898–1956)... 'in the dark times / will there also be dancing?'[387] Dancing about the dark times, but dancing none-the-less.

---

385 Patton. *Man's Hidden Search* 110.
386 Crosby. *More than Discourses*, 91.
387 The original line is: in the dark times / will there also be singing? The line appears in Brecht's 1938 *Svendborg Poems*, which he wrote while in exile in Denmark.

Some 'Take-Aways' from Bernard Eugene Meland

"The structure of Christian faith is symphonic rather than logical."

"The distinctive religious dimension... is awareness and appreciation of reality. Religion is reality-centering."

"If the history of doctrines and of philosophy reveals anything, it is that concepts and doctrines are, at best, but approximations to the truth of things. It cannot be otherwise."

"We must acknowledge ourselves creatures of earth, whose air we breathe, by whose herbs we are nourished, and by whose water we are refreshed and sustained."

"The attitude of reverence should temper intellectual differences among us. Nothing is more disconcerting that the ruthless disregard which religious people show for one another in their theological disagreements."

"What's needed in theology today and, in fact, throughout all our thinking: a blending of the scientific and the poetic feel for life."

"One can never identify the religious objective with what is institutionally fixed."

"Art, whether it expresses itself through music, poetry, painting, or architecture, presents the common stuff of experience in uncommon ways, made possible by the genius of a sensitive imagination."

"Without appreciative awareness, religion can degenerate into a pathological concern for salvation from sin."

"... there is something about church Christianity that depresses the creativities of men, that foreshortens their imaginative and critical powers and impels them to suspect concern with qualitative attainment, thus lulling them into or even summoning them to a preference for mediocrity."

"The tragedy of supernaturalism has been that it has lured man away from the universe. It has left him hostile, fearsome, or indifferent to the great life that surges through him and through his fellow creatures."

"The conviction that 'the earth is actually and literally the mother of us all' is the beginning of a mystical naturalism and the basis for a new theistic worship."

"All the rare achievements of personality – integrity, friendliness, understanding, deep sympathy, gratitude, and reverence – are the flowerings of social interaction carried on at the human level. Thus man, even in his spiritual behavior, is an expression of earth forces. He is, as it has been said, the universe come to consciousness."

Combined Bibliography

A

Abbott, M. *Cosmic Sparks. Igniting a Re-Enchantment with the Sacred.* Bayswater. Coventry Press, 2020

Abbott, S. "Tasmania's Top 200 Giant Trees Registered, Mapped and Open for business". *ABC News.* ABC Northern Tasmania. 4 August 2020. (Accessed 12 December 2020)

Abram, D. *The Spell of the Sensuous. Perception and Language in a More-Than-Human World.* Twentieth Anniversary Edition. New York. Vintage Books 1996, 2017

Alexander, S. *Beauty and Other Forms of Value.* London. Macmillan, 1933

Alves, R. A. *The Poet The Warrior The Prophet.* The Edward Cadbury Lectures 1990. Philadelphia. SCM/Trinity Press International, 1990

————, *A Theology of Human Hope.* Washington: Corpus Books, 1969

Austin, R. C. *Baptised into Wilderness. A Christian Perspective on John Muir.* Atlanta. John Knox, 1987

Axel, L. E. "Reshaping the Task of Theology" in William Dean (ed.) *The Size of God. The Theology of Bernard Loomer in Context*, in *American Journal of Theology & Philosophy* 8, 1 & 2, January & May 1987

B

Baird, J. *Phosphorescence. On Awe, Wonder and Things that Sustain you when the World goes Dark.* Sydney. Fourth Estate/HarperCollins, 2020

Barrett, J. E. "Pragmatism, Process, and Courage" in W. C. Peden & L. E. Axel (eds). *New Essays in Religious Naturalism.*

Highlands Institute Series 2. Georgia. Mercer University Press, 1993

Berry, T, "The Universe Manifests the Sacred" in Thomas Berry. *Selected Writings on the Earth Community*. Selected with Introduction by M. E. Tucker & J. Grim. Maryknoll. Orbis Books, 2014

_____, "A Cosmological Understanding of the Trinity" in Thomas Berry. *Selected Writings on the Earth Community*. Selected with Introduction by M. E. Tucker & J. Grim. Maryknoll. Orbis Books, 2014

_____ -, "Human Intimacy with Earth" in Thomas Berry. *Selected Writings on the Earth Community*. Selected with Introduction by M. E. Tucker & J. Grim. Maryknoll. Orbis Books, 2014

_____, "Sacred Moments" in Mary E Tucker & John Grim. (ed). Thomas Berry: *Selected Writings on the Earth Community*. Selected with Introduction by M. E. Tucker & J. Grim. Maryknoll. Orbis Books, 2014

_____, "The Christian Future and the Fate of the Earth" in Thomas Berry. *Selected Writings on the Earth Community*. Selected with Introduction by M. E. Tucker & J. Grim. Maryknoll, Orbis Books, 2014

_____, *The Sacred Universe. Earth, Spirituality, and Religion in the Twenty-First Century*. (ed.) Mary E. Tucker. New York. Columbia University Press, 2009

_____, *The Great Work. Our Way into the Future*. New York. Harmony/Bell Tower, 1999

Bessler, J. A. *A Scandalous Jesus. How Three Historic Quests Changed Theology for the Better*. Salem. Polebridge, 2013

Brack, C. & M. Brookhouse. "Where the Old Things Are: Australia's Most Ancient Trees". *The Conversation*, ABC, 19 April 2017. (Accessed 3 September 2018)

Braxton, D. M. "Sacrament and Sacrifice: The Feedback Loops of Religious Community" in P. Clayton (ed.) *Arthur Peacock: All That Is. A Naturalistic Faith for the Twenty-First Century*. Minneapolis. Fortress Press, 2007

Bridle, J. *Ways of Being. Beyond Human Intelligence.* (Global). Allen Lane/Penguin, 2022

Brown, A. J. "Encounter - A Religious Naturalist 'Road to Damascus' Experience". Sermon. Memorial Unitarian Church, Cambridge, UK. 20 January 2019

Brune, M. "All the Colors of Nature". *Coming Clean Blog*, 12 November 2015. Republished in John Muir Exhibit. https:vault.sierraclub.org/john_muir_exhibit/life/all_the_colors_of_nature_michael_brune.aspx (Accessed 3 June 2021)

Brussatt, F. "An Interview with Sam Keen". *Spirituality & Practice*, https://www.spiritualityandpractice.com/books/features/view/17541/an-interview-with-sam-keen (Accessed 18/2/2020)

Bumbaugh, D. "Toward a Humanist Vocabulary of Reverence". *Boulder International Humanist Institute, Fourth Annual Symposium*, Boulder, Colorado. 22 February 2003. (Accessed 20 December 2015). <http://www.uua.org/sites/live-new.uua.org/files/documents/bumbaughdavid/>

_____, "Flower Communion Service" and "A Springtime Service" in C. Seaburg. (ed). *The Communion Book*. Boston. UUMA, 1993.

Burns, S. *Worship and Ministry. Shaped Towards God.* Preston. Mosaic Press, 2012

_____, "Over the Ocean" in S. Burns & A. Monro (eds) *Christian Worship in Australia. Inculturating the Liturgical Tradition.* Strathfield. St Paul's, 2009

C

Campbell, S-E. (ed.) *The Face of the Earth. Natural Landscapes, Science, and Culture.* Berkeley. University of California Press, 2011

Carson, R. *Silent Spring.* New York. Houghton Mifflin, 1962

———, *The Sense of Wonder. A Celebration of Nature for Parents and Children.* New York. Harper Perennial, 1956

Collins, P. "Religion is Poetry or it is Nothing!". *ABC Religion & Ethics.* 10 December 2010

Colloff, M. *Landscapes of our Hearts. Reconciling People and Environment.* Port Melbourne. Thames & Hudson, 2020/2023

Comins, M. *A Wild Faith. Jewish Ways into Wilderness, Wilderness Ways into Judaism.* Jewish Lights Publishing, 2007/2014 Second Printing

Coots, M. *Seasons of the Self.* Nashville. Abingdon, 1971

Crawford, B. "The Majesty of Trees. Celebrating the Season of Creation." https://thesouloftheearth.com/

Crosby, D. A. *More Than Discourse. Symbolic Expressions of Naturalistic Faith.* New York. State University of New York, 2014

D

Dartnell, L. *Origins. How the Earth Shaped Human History.* London. Vintage, 2019

De Cruz, H. "The Necessity of Awe". *Aeon Newsletter*, 10 July 2020. (Accessed 15 July 2020)

Dowd, M. *Thank God for Evolution. How the Marriage of Science and Religion will Transform your Life and our World.* New York. Plume, 2009

E

Eaton, H. "Beauty Will Save The World". *Counterpoint Navigating Knowledge Blog*, 30 June 2021

Elias, A. "Useless Beauty: Re-Politicising Australian Wildflowers" Sydney Environment Institute, 4 September 2019

Eliot, T. S. *"The Waste Land"*. 1922. *Poetry Foundation*. <https://www.poetryfoundation.org/poems/47311/the-waste-land>

F

Farrier, D. "Wild Clocks" in *Emergence Magazine*, 23 January 2025. (Accessed 24 January 2025)

Fleischman, P. R. *Wonder. When and Why the World Appears Radiant*. Amherst. Small Batch Books, 2013

Fox, M. et al. *Order of the Sacred Earth. An Intergenerational Vision of Love and Action*. New York. Monkfish Book Publishing, 2018

Frank, A. "Whither Wonder?" in *Orbiter*, 2 October 2019. (Accessed 18 October 2019)

———, "Wilderness in Everywhere" in *Orbiter*, 19 February 2019. (Accessed 21 December 2019)

Frank, A. F "Climate Change and the Power of Story", *Orbiter Magazine*, 26 June 2018. (Accessed 1 January 2020)

Franklin, R. "What Mary Oliver's Critic Don't Understand". *The New Yorker*. Books. 20 November 2017. <https://www.newyorker.com/magazine/2017/11/27/what-mary-olivers-critics-dont-understand>

Funk, R. "Editorial" in *The Fourth R* 18, 1, (2005), 2, 20

G

Gagen, M. "Why Keeping One Mature Street Tree is far Better for Humans and Nature than Planting lots of New Ones". https://phys.org/news/2021-02-mature... Republished by

The Conversation. 2 February 2021. (Accessed 9 February 2021)

Galston, D. "The Historical Jesus is not the Christ". *Westar Institute Blog*. 27 September 2023

_____, "McJesus". *Westar Institute. Biblical and Theological Reflections Blog*, 17 January 2019

_____, *Embracing the Human Jesus. A Wisdom Path for Contemporary Christianity*. Salem. Polebridge Press, 2012

_____, "Liturgy in the Key of Q" in D. Galston. *Embracing the Human Jesus. A Wisdom Path for Contemporary Christianity*. Salem. Polebridge Press, 2012

Geering, L. G. *From the Big Bang to God. Our Awe-Inspiring Journey of Evolution*. Salem. Polebridge Press, 2013

_____, *Coming Back to Earth. From gods, to God, to Gaia*. Salem. Polebridge Press, 2010

_____, *The Greening of Christianity*. Wellington. St Andrew's Trust, 2005

Gillett, P. R. "Theology Of, By, and For Religious Naturalism" in *Journal of Liberal Religion* 6, 1, 2006, 1-6.

Gleiser, M. "I Wonder as I Wander" in *Orbiter*, 12 December 2019. (Accessed 21 December 2019)

_____, *The Simple Beauty of the Unexpected. A Natural Philosopher's Quest for Trout and the Meaning of Everything*. Lebanon NH: ForeEdge, 2016

Goodenough, U. *The Sacred Depths of Nature. How Life has Emerged and Evolved*. Second Edition. New York. Oxford University Press, 2023

_____, "Taking Nature to Mind and Heart" A paper presented at the 'Naturalism – as Religion, within Religions, or without Religion?', *IRAS Conference 2021* at Star Island, Sunday 27 June–Saturday 3 July, 2021

———, "Honouring Nature All the Way Down" in *Journal for the Study of Religion, Nature and Culture* 9, 2, 176-180, 2015

———, "Vertical and Horizontal Transcendence" in *Zygon* 36, 1, (March 2001), 21-31

———, *The Sacred Depths of Nature*. New York. Oxford University Press, 1998.

Goodenough, U. & T. W. Deacon. "The Sacred Emergence of Nature" in P. Clayton. (ed.) *The Oxford Handbook of Religion and Science*. London. Oxford University Press, 2007

H

Habel, N. C. *Rainbow of Mysteries. Meeting the Sacred in Nature*. Kelowna. Copperhouse, 2012

———, *An Inconvenient Text*. Adelaide. ATF Press, 2009

Hanh, Thich Nhat. "Present Moment Wonderful Moment" in E. Roberts & E. Amidon. *Life Prayers from Around the World. 365 Prayers, Blessings, and Affirmations to Celebrate the Human Journey*. New York. HarperCollins, 1996

Hare, W. "Dug up in Australia, burned around the World - exporting fossil fuels undermines climate targets". *The Conversation*, 13 August 2024

Haskell, D. G. "Listening and the Crisis of Inattention". *Emergence (On-line) Magazine*. 21 April 2022. (Accessed 11 August 2023) <https://emergencemagazine.org>

Hedrick, C. W. *The Wisdom of Jesus. Between the Sages of Israel and the Apostles of the Church*. Eugene. Cascade Books, 2014

Hefner, P. "Forward" in J. A. Stone. *Religious Naturalism Today. The Rebirth of a Forgotten Alternative*. New York. State University of New York, 2008

Heschel, A. J. *God in Search of Man. A Philosophy of Judaism.* New York. Farrar, Straus & Giroux, (1955) Reprint 1976

Highland, C. "John Muir's Radical Religion of Beauty". *The Humanist*, 1-5, 27 December 2019

Hogue, M. S. "Religion Without God: The Way of Religious Naturalism" in *The Fourth R* 27, 3, (May-June 2014), 3-6, 15-16

_____, *The Promise of Religious Naturalism.* Maryland. Rowman & Littlefield, 2010

Horne, J. *The Pursuit of Wonder. How Australia's Landscape was Explored, Nature Discovered and Tourism Unleased.* Carlton, The Miegunyah Press, 2005

Horsfield, P. *From Jesus to the Internet. A History of Christianity and Media.* West Sussex. Wiley Blackwell, 2015

Hughes, L. "Aim Higher, Act Faster, or Risk Losing it All': Climate Change Report Offers 'final warning'. *The New Daily*, 19 March 2023. (Accessed 20 March 2023)

Hunt, R. A. E. "In Celebration of a 'Wild' Faith: Jesus in the Australian Landscape" in G. C. Jenks (ed). *Interfaith Afterlives of Jesus. Jesus in Global Perspective 2*. Westar Studies. Eugene. Cascade Books, 2023

_____, *Seasons and Self. Discourses on Being 'at home' in Nature.* Bayswater. Coventry Press, 2018

_____, *When Progressives Gather Together. Liturgy, Lectionary, Landscape... And Other Explorations.* Northcote. Morning Star, 2016

_____, "Please Tell Us Your Stories: Reimagining the Poetic in Religious Communication" in *Proceedings... Faith, Story, and Community.* (ed) H. M. Sterk & W. Thorn. Marquette University. Milwaukee, Wisconsin, 1993.

I

Inbody, T. *The Constructive Theology of Bernard Meland. Postliberal Empirical Realism.* Georgia. Scholars Press, 1995

———, "Bernard Meland: 'A Rebel Among Process Theologians'" in *American Journal of Theology and Philosophy* 5, 2 & 3 (May and September) 1984, 43-71

J

"John Muir: A Brief Biography". Sierra Club - *John Muir Biography*. https:vault.sierraclub.org/john_muir_exhibit/life/muir_biography.aspx (Accessed 1 June 2021)

"John Muir in Australia". Sierra Club - *John Muir Exhibit*. https:vault.sierraclub.org/john_muir_exhibit/geography/australia/default.aspx (Accessed 1 June 2021)

Johnson, C. V. "Relating Liturgical Time to 'place-time': The Spatiotemporal Dislocation of the Liturgical Year in Australia" in S. Burns & A. Monro (eds) *Christian Worship in Australia. Inculturating the Liturgical Tradition.* Strathfield. St Paul's Publications, 2009

Johnson, E. "Deep Incarnation: Prepare to be Astonished", UNIFAS Conference, Rio de Janeiro, (7-14 July 2010). <https://sgfp.wordpress.com/2011/02/15/deep-incarnation-prepare-to-be-astonished/> (Accessed 4 October 2016)

K

Karskens, G. *People of the River. Lost Worlds of Early Australia.* Melbourne. Allen & Unwin, 2020

———, *The Colony. A History of Early Sydney.* Crows Nest. Allen & Unwin, 2009

Keefe-Perry, L. B. C. *Way to Water. A Theopoetics Primer.* Eugene. Wipf & Stock, 2014

_____, "Theopoetics: Process and Perspective" in *Christianity and Literature* 58, 4, (Summer 2009), 579-601

Keen, S. *Apology for Wonder*. New York. Harper & Row, 1969

Keltner, D. et al. "Awe, the Diminished Self, and Collective Engagement: Universals and Cultural Variations in the Small Self". *American Psychological Association*, 2017

_____, "Why Do We Feel Awe?" in *Mind & Body*. 10 May 2016. (Accessed 23 September 2019)

Keneally, Thomas. *Australians. Origins to Eureka*. Volume 1. Crows Nest. Allen & Unwin, 2009.

King, E. W. "A Pastoral Theological Reflection on Storytelling" in *Chicago Studies* 21, 1, 7-21, 1982

Kimmerer, R. W. "The Intelligence of Plants". A radio script from *On Being* with Krista Tippett. Air date: 25 February 2016. Updated: 12 May 2022. (Accessed 30 May 2022)

_____, *Braiding Sweetgrass. Indigenous Wisdom, Scientific Knowledge and the Teachings of Plants*. London. Penguin Random House, 2013

L

LaChapelle, D. "Ritual is Essential: Seeing Ritual and Ceremony as Sophisticated Social and Spiritual Technology". One of the articles in *Art And Ceremony In Sustainable Culture* (IC#5) Originally published in Spring 1984. (c)1984, 1997 by Context Institute.

Lau, G. "Reflections on the Pale Blue Dot". *Orbiter*, 23 October 2019. (Accessed 26 October 2019).

Lawrie, C. "Baptism. A Reflection", *The Age*, 7 November 2009

Limbaugh, R. H.. "The Nature of John Muir's Religion", *The Pacific Historian* 29, 2 & 3, Summer/Fall, 1985, 16-30

Loehr, D.. "Salvation by Character: How UU's can find the Religious Center" in *Journal of Liberal Religion* 1, 2, 1-14, 2000

Logan, J. "The Resurgence of Life". *Poetry Soup*. 22 March 2021 <https://www.poetrysoup.com/poem/resurgence_of_life_1340115>

London, S. "Renewing Our Sense of Wonder: An Interview with Sam Keen". (This interview was adapted from the public radio series *"Insight & Outlook."* It was published in the October 1999 issue of *The Sun* magazine under the title "On the Flying Trapeze: Sam Keen Ponders How to Be Free." https://scott.london/interviews/keen.html (Accessed 2/2/2020)

Loorz, V. *Church of the Wild. How Nature Invites Us into the Sacred*. Minneapolis, Broadleaf Books, 2021

M

McCarthy, M. "Nature, Joy, and Human Becoming". An *On Being* interview with Krista Tippett. Original air time: 3 May 2018. Updated: 27 August 2020. (Accessed 7 November 2022)

McRae-McMahon, D. *Rituals for Life, Love and Loss*. Paddington. Jane Curry Publishing, 2003

Macrae, A. "Why I am Returning my AO Honour", *Crosslight* 28 January 2021

Mahany, B. *The Book of Nature. The Astonishing Beauty of God's First Sacred Text*. Minneapolis. Broadleaf Books, 2023

Matthews, C. *The Celtic Book of Days. A Celebration of Celtic Wisdom*. New Alresford. Godsfield Press, 1995

Mayer, P. Comment in Living the Questions. (DVD Series). *Pro-Future Faith. The Prodigal Species Comes Home*, 2020

"Meaning and Symbolism of Hyacinth". *Teleflora*. n.d. <https://www.teleflora.com/meaning-of-flowers/hyacinth?promotion=AUGUSTWELCOME5>

Meland, B. E. "Fifty Years of Religious Inquiry" (1979) in W. C. Peden. *Life and Thought of Bernard Eugene Meland, American Constructive Theologian, 1899–1993*. Newcastle upon Tyne. Cambridge Scholars Publishing, 2010

———, *Fallible Forms and Symbols. Discourses of Method in a Theology of Culture*. Philadelphia. Fortress Press, 1976

———, "Grace: A Dimension within Nature", *Journal of Religion* 54, 2, (April 1974), 119-137

———, *Higher Education and the Human Spirit*. Chicago. University of Chicago Press, 1953.

———, *Faith and Culture*. New York. Oxford University Press, 1953

———, *The Reawakening of Christian Faith*. New York. Books for Libraries Press 1949/(Reprint 1972)

———, "Art, Religion and the Cultural Mood" (1946) published in J. N. Gaston & W. C. Peden (eds). *Bernard Eugene Meland's Unpublished Papers*, Newcastle upon Tyne. Cambridge Scholars Publishing. 2013

———, "Mysticism in Modern Terms" (1939) published in J. N. Gaston & W. C. Peden (eds). *Bernard Eugene Meland's Unpublished Papers*, Newcastle upon Tyne. Cambridge Scholars Publishing. 2013

———, "Religion Rooted in Nature" (1938) published in J. N. Gaston & W. C. Peden (eds). *Bernard Eugene Meland's Unpublished Papers*, Newcastle upon Tyne. Cambridge Scholars Publishing. 2013

———, "The Mystic Returns", *Journal of Religion* 17, 2, (1937), 146-160. (Accessed 18/7/2020)

———, *Modern Man's Worship. A Search for Reality in Religion*. New York. Harper & Brothers, 1934

———, "Kinsmen of the Wild. Religious Moods in Modern American Poetry". *The Sewanee Review* 41, (1933) 443-453. (Accessed 16/6/2020)

———, "The Worship Mood" in *Religious Education* 26, 8, (October 1931), 661-665

Merton, T. *When the Trees Say Nothing. Writings on Nature*. K. Deignan (ed.). Notre Dame, Sorin Books/Ave Maria Press, 2015

Miller., R. J. "Free Rain", *The Fourth R* 34, 1. January-February 2021, 1

Monahan, J. "Bite into Poetry..." *The Ledger*. January 2005. <https://www.theledger.com/article/LK/20050111/News/608089277/LL>

Morgan, J. & G. Garrett. *On The Edge: A-Way with the Ocean*. Reservoir. Morning Star Publishing, 2018

Moring, M. "Don't Do Awe Alone. Here's Why?" *Orbiter*. 10 August 2017

N

Newell, J. P. *Sacred Earth, Sacred Soul. A Celtic Guide to Listening to our Souls and Saving the World*. London. William Collins, 2021

Nickerson, B. *Celebrate the Sun. A Heritage of Festivals Interpreted Through the Art of Children from Many Lands*. Philadelphia. J B Lippincott Co., 1969

O

O'Donohue, J. *Walking in Wonder. Eternal Wisdom for the Modern World*. In Conversation with John Quinn. New York. Convergent, 2015

_____, *Four Elements. Reflections on Nature.* New York. Harmony Press, 2010

_____-, "The Inner Landscape of Beauty". *On Being* broadcast with Krista Tippett. 26 February 2008. Updated 31 August 2017

_____, *Eternal Echoes. Exploring our Hunger to Belong.* London. Bantam Press, 1998

_____, *Anam Cara. Spiritual Wisdom from the Celtic World.* London. Bantam Press, 1997

O'Murchu, D. *Ecological Spirituality.* Maryknoll, Orbis Books, 2024

Oliver, M. "When I am Among the Trees". 2019. https://apoemaday.tumblr.com/post/189705365465/when-i-am-among-the-trees

_____, *Evidence: Poems.* Reprint Edition. Boston. Beacon Press, 2010

_____, *New and Selected Poems.* Boston. Beacon, 1992

Orr, D. *Down to the Wire: Confronting Climate Collapse.* Oxford. Oxford University, 2009

P

Palka, J. "Nature is Rising", *Nature's Depths*, <https://naturesdepths.com/> 16 April 2023

_____, "A Banquet for Butterflies and Bumblebees" 30 August 2020. <https://naturesdepths.com/>

_____, "Valuing Nature" (https://naturedepths.com/) June 2018

_____, "Is Earth Alive?" in *Nature's Depths* (https://naturesdepths.com/), 5 March 2017

_____, "To See a World in a Grain of Sand". 15 November 2015. <https://naturesdepth.com/>

Bibliography

Pascoe, B. *Black Duck. A Year at Yumburra*. (With Lyn Harwood). Cremorne. Thames & Hudson 2024

Patton, K. L. *Man's Hidden Search. An Inquiry into Naturalistic Mysticism*. Boston. Meeting House Press/Beacon Press, 1954

Pearce, J. et al. "What Fosters Awe-inspiring Experiences in Nature-based Tourism Destinations?". *Journal of Sustainable Tourism* 25, 3, 362-378. Published through the Murdoch Research Repository, Murdoch University

Peden, W. C. *Life and Thought of Bernard Eugene Meland American Constructive Theologian 1899-1993*. New York. Cambridge Scholars Publishing, 2010

_____, *The Chicago School. Voices in Liberal Religious Thought*. Wyndham Hall Press, 1987

Peters, K. E. *Christian Naturalism. Christian Thinking for Living in This World Only*. Eugene. Wipf & Stock, 2022

_____, "Human Salvation in an Evolutionary Worldview: An Exploration in Christian Naturalism" in *Zygon* 47, 4, (December 2012), 843-869

_____, "Empirical Theology and a 'Naturalistic Christian Faith'" in P. Clayton (ed) *Arthur Peacock: All That Is. A Naturalistic Faith for the Twenty-First Century*. Minneapolis. Fortress Press, 2007

_____, *Dancing with the Sacred. Evolution, Ecology, and God*. Harrisburg. Trinity Press International, 2002

_____, "Storytellers and Scenario Spinners: Some Reflections on Religion and Science in Light of a Pragmatic, Evolutionary Theory of Knowledge", in *Zygon: Journal of Religion and Science* 32, 4, (December 1997), 465-489.

_____, "Interrelating Nature, Humanity, and the Work of God: Some Issues for Future Reflection" in *Zygon:*

Journal of Religion and Science 27, 4, (December 1992), 403-419

Primack, J. R. & N. E. Abrams. *The View from the Centre of the Universe. Discovering our Extraordinary Place in the Cosmos*. New York. Riverhead Books, 2006

R

Ranson, D. "Fire in Water. The Liturgical Cycle in the Experience of South East Australian Seasonal Patterns" in *Compass Theology Review* 26, 1992

Raymo, C. "My Very Distant Cousin, the Turnip". *Science Musings*. Originally written 14 October 1985. Blogged 6 August 2019. (Accessed 10 February 2020)

Ricoeur, P. "Biblical Hermeneutics" in *Semeia*, 4, 29-148, 1975

Robbins, J. "Ecopsychology: How Immersion in Nature Benefits your Health". *Yale Environment 360*. 9 January 2020. (Accessed 17 January 2020)

Rose, D. B. "On The Spot: In The Red Centre" in S-E. Campbell, *The Face of the Earth. Natural Landscapes, Science, and Culture*. Berkeley. University of California, 2011

Rue, L. *Religion is Not About God. How Spiritual Traditions Nurture our Biological Nature and What to Expect When they Fail*. New Brunswick. Rutgers University Press, 2006

Ryan, P. J. "John Muir and the Tall Trees of Australia", *The Pacific Historian* 29, 2 & 3, Summer/Fall, 1985, 125-136

S

Sagan, C. *The Varieties of Scientific Experience. A Personal View of the Search for God*. (ed.) Ann Druyan. New York. Penguin, 2006

Sanders, S. R. "Useless Beauty: A Canticle for the Cosmos." 2012. Re-published in *Notre Dame Magazine*, 2020. (Accessed May 2020)

Sanguin, B. "Cosmic Sacrifice" and "Feast of the Cosmos" in *If Darwin Prayed: Prayers for Evolutionary Mystics*. Vancouver. ES Press, 2010

⸺, *Darwin, Divinity, and the Dance of The Cosmos. An Ecological Christianity*. Kelowna. Copper House/Wood Lake Publishing, 2007

Scott, B. B. "Blowin' in the Wind". *Westar Institute Blog*. 2 February 2023

Seaburg, C. (ed.) *The Communion Book. An Anthology*. Boston. Unitarian Universalist Ministers Association, 1993

Shaver, R. E. "In Awe of Dying Leaves". A sermon delivered at First Church of Christ, Congregational, United Church of Christ, in North Conway, New Hampshire. USA. 11 November 2019. (Accessed 22 November 2019)

Shaw, M. C. *Nature's Grace. Essays on H. N. Wieman's Finite Theism*. New York. Peter Lang, 1995

Shore, S. B. "It's Earth Day, Let's Celebrate Ourselves!" Sermon. Unitarian Universalist Church of Asheville, 23 April 2006

Sideris, L. H. "Science as Sacred Myth? Ecospirituality in the Anthropocene Age." *Journal for the Study of Religion, Nature and Culture* 9, 2. 2015. 136-153

Siedenburg, K. *Space Between the Stones. Poetry & Practices for Connecting with Nature, Spirit, and Creativity*. Santa Cruz. Our Nature Connection, 2020

⸺, *Poems of Earth and Spirit. 70 Poems and 40 Practices to Deepen Your Connection with Nature*. Santa Cruz. Our Nature Connection, 2017

Smith, D. E. & H. E. Taussig. *Many Tables. The Eucharist in the New Testament and Liturgy Today*. Eugene. Wipf & Stock, 2001

Solnit, R. "Every Time you Commit an Antisocial Act, Push an Acorn into the Ground". On Orwell's lessons from Nature. *The Guardian*. 16 October 2021 (Accessed 17 October 2021)

Spirn, A. W. "Constructing Nature: The Legacy of Frederick Law Olmsted" in W. Cronon. *Uncommon Ground. ReThinking the Human Place in Nature*. New York. W. W. Norton, 1996

Stillwater, J. D. "The Awe of an Eclipse". *Religious Naturalist Association Newsletter*, April 2024

Stone, J. A. *Sacred Nature. The Environmental Potential of Religious Naturalism*. London. Routledge, 2017

_____, *Religious Naturalism Today. The Rebirth of a Forgotten Alternative*. New York. State University of New York, 2008

_____, "Inaugural Liberal Arts Lecture", 1998, William Harper College, Chicago, quoted in M. S. Hogue. *The Promise of Religious Naturalism*. Lanham. Rowman & Littlefield, 2010

Suttie, J. "Why Trees can Make you Happier". *Mind and Body*. 26 April 2019. (Accessed 29 September 2019)

_____, "Why is Nature so Good for your Mental Health?" in *Mind & Body*. 19 April 2019. (Accessed 23 September 2019)

Suzuki, D. & A. McConnell. *The Sacred Balance. Rediscovering our Place in Nature*. Sydney. Allen & Unwin, 1997

Swimme B. T. & M. E. Tucker. *Journey of the Universe*. New Haven. Yale University Press, 2011

T

Tacey, D. *The Spirituality Revolution. The Emergence of Contemporary Spirituality*. Pymble. HarperCollins, 2003

———, *ReEnchantment. The New Australian Spirituality*. Pymble. HarperCollins, 2000

Tallmadge, J. "John Muir and the Poetics of Natural Conversion". n.d. Pages: 62-79. Original in University of Michigan. Digitized by Google

The St Hilda Community. *The New Women Included. A Book of Services and Prayers*. London. SPCK, 1996

Tippett, K. "Listening to the World: Mary Oliver". *Radio 'On Being' Interview*, 5 February 2015. Updated 17 January 2019

———, "Forward", in J. O'Donohue. *Walking in Wonder. Eternal Wisdom for a Modern World*. In Conversation with John Quinn. New York. Convergent, 2015

Towne, E. A. "God and the Chicago School in the Theology of Bernard E. Meland" in *American Journal of Theology & Philosophy* 10, 1, (January 1989), 3-19

U

Ungunmerr-Baumann, M-R. *Living Water*, Blog, 26 January 2021. <https://www.thelivingwater.com.au/blog/dadirri-our-greatest-gift-to-australia-says-indigenous-elder-and-2021-senior-australian-of-the-year>

UUA Worship Web. Boston. <www.uua.org/spirituallife/worshipweb/>

V

Vearncombe, E. et al. (eds). *After Jesus Before Christianity. A Historical Exploration of the First Two Centuries of Jesus Movements*. New York. HarperOne, 2021

Vogt, V. O. *Modern Worship*. Lowell Institute Lectures. New Haven. Yale University, 1927

Vosper, G. *Amen. What Prayer Can Mean in a World Beyond Belief*. Toronto. HarperCollins, 2012

————, *We All Breathe. Poems and Prayers*. Toronto. PostPurgical Resources, 2012

————, *With or Without God. Why the Way we Live is More Important than What we Believe*. Toronto. HarperCollins, 2008

W

Webb, V. *Stepping Out with the Sacred. Human Attempts to Engage the Divine*. London. Continuum International, 2010

Weston, R. T. "Out of the Stars". No. 530, in *Singing The Living Tradition*. Boston. Unitarian Universalist Association, 1993

Westerhoff, J. H. "Contemporary Spirituality: Revelation, Myth and Ritual" in G. Durka & J. Smith (eds). *Aesthetic Dimensions of Religious Education*. New York. Paulist Press, 1979

White, J. F. *The Sacraments in Protestant Practice and Faith*. Nashville. Abingdon Press, 1999

White, S. J. *Christian Worship and Technological Change*. Nashville. Abingdon, 1994

Wieman, H. N. & B. E Meland. *American Philosophies of Religion*. New York. Willets, Clark & Co. 1936

Wilder, A. N. *Theopoetic. Theology and the Religious Imagination*. Philadelphia. Fortress Press, 1976

Williamson, C. M. "Bernard E. Meland: What Kind of Theologian?", in *Process Studies* 5, 4, (Winter 1975) 369-390

Winton, T. *The Land's Edge*. Sydney. Picador, 1993

Wohlleben, P. *The Hidden Life of Trees. What They Feel, How They Communicate: Discoveries from a Secret World*. London. William Collins, 2016

Wulf, A. *The Invention of Nature. Alexander von Humboldt's New World*. New York. Vintage Books, 2015

www.ingramcontent.com/pod-product-compliance
Lightning Source LLC
Chambersburg PA
CBHW011127070526
44584CB00028B/3804